Praise for Beverly A. Hall's

Surviving and Thriving After a Life Threatening Diagnosis

This book is written by an extraordinary individual who combines the wisdom gained from the personal experiences of a life-threatening diagnosis, and the skills of a highly credentialed medical professional. Beverly has guided her life through a combination of wise common sense about daily living with the ability to make the best use of modern science. This book redefines a life threatening diagnosis as a wake-up call to live fully. It should be read by everyone long before they have a life-threatening diagnosis.

Robert M. Duggan, *President, Tai Sophia Institute for the Healing Arts, Laurel, Maryland*

SURVIVING AND THRIVING is a courageous exploration of survival and of the path to developing a thriving life that will have an enormous impact on anyone who is dealing with a serious illness. This book invites the reader to look at life threatening illness in an entirely different way and to develop a life affirming new perspective. Beverly Hall speaks as a survivor and as highly educated health professional. This book provides each reader with the power, ability and wisdom to find and use the sources of health and healing within each of us.

Janet D. Allan, PhD, RN, FAAN, *Professor and Dean, University of Maryland School of Nursing*

This book could simply be titled: "How to Survive and Thrive." It is a book for everyone, whether you have received a life-threatening diagnosis, or whether you have yet to receive one. Beverly Hall has written from her own personal experience as a cancer survivor, a nurse. a researcher, and a university professor. I will pass this book along to every one of my friends and colleagues, inviting them to also join in this important journey.

Peggy L. Chinn, PhD, RN, FAAN, *Editor, <u>Advances in Nursing Sciences</u> and Professor Emeria, University of Connecticut*

Here is a book that speaks to "all" of me: to the survivor of two life-threatening events; to the nurse concerned with caring for people with life-threatening events; to the public health professional who focuses on prevention; and to the educator wanting to provide my 'audience' with accurate and relevant information. This is it! Beverly Hall has provided us with a lucid, practical guide to health. This is information for everyone who wants to take charge of their lives. It is something that will be an important part of my own practice and my own self healing.

Elizabeth (Bets) Anderson, DrPH, RN, FAAN, *Professor, University of Texas Medical Branch.*

SURVIVING AND THRIVING AFTER A LIFE-THREATENING DIAGNOSIS

Second Edition

Beverly A. Hall, PhD, RN, FAAN

authorHOUSE®

AuthorHouse™
1663 Liberty Drive, Suite 200
Bloomington, IN 47403
www.authorhouse.com
Phone: 1-800-839-8640

First published by AuthorHouse   8/11/2008

ISBN: 978-1-4343-9550-4 (sc)

Library of Congress Control Number: 2008905398

Printed in the United States of America
Bloomington, Indiana

This book is printed on acid-free paper.

This book is dedicated to my great friend and colleague, Dr. Janet Allan, and to all the clients, family members, friends, colleagues, and friends of friends with cancer and HIV who, over the years, have exchanged health information with me, and have started their own journey toward high level health. You have been such an inspiration in my life.

I also dedicate this edition to the people who wrote or called after reading the first edition of *Surviving and Thriving*. When I wrote the book I reasoned that if it helped just one person, it would be worth all the time and energy spent on its construction. It has done far more than that. Some of you purchased 10-30 copies to give to friends and family. Others have written about specific chapters, such as prayer, meditation, or nutrition that you felt helped you turn around your illness and your attitude toward a positive direction. May you receive this next edition on the wings of my love and gratitude.

Contents

Introduction

Freedom Is Another Word For Nothing Left To Lose

None of us survivors will ever forget the day, hour, and minute that a doctor informed us that in a shorter order than we had ever dreamed possible, our very lives might come to an end. Twenty five years ago this happened to me. I became numb all over. My insides felt hollow, empty. I could barely stand up as I walked outside into the bleak San Francisco fog, perfect weather for the dying person that I was. A few hours before, I had been grumbling about a shivering head cold and the bitter, windy weather. Now I could barely feel the temperature. And my cold...well, what an insignificant inconvenience that turned out to be. This beclouded, depressed, terrified, and uncanny feeling was my enemy for many weeks.

If this is how you feel right now, I want to grab you and hold you close while you listen to me. I want to talk directly into your ear as I tell you that this is not the beginning of the end, no matter how much you may think it is. I want to speak about preposterous things to you - for one, that this is the beginning of a new turn in your beautiful life where you will get a chance to learn the thriving skills that follow a life-threatening diagnosis - that after awhile, you will be telling other people that you have never been happier. And I want you to know that when you start on this journey, you will no longer be worried about illness or God forbid - death. Instead, you will be living. In your transformation into being a living person, you will, well...how can I say it better...you will live.

News about any health problem, even minor ones, such as sports-related injuries, can set us back tremendously, because they bring on a sense of futility and loss of control. Before, we were always able to count on the fact that our bodies would perform whatever we patiently demanded from them. So, almost everyone has had some experience that allows them to understand how a serious health problem would have a very huge impact on emotional health. The body, always taken for granted, has turned against you. It now cannot be counted on to be fit and sustain life. What can you trust?

It is just this state of mind, the condition of mistrust that is set up between the mind and the body that fuels morbid prophesies about our prognosis in life-threatening disease. When someone tells you that you have such a serious disease that you could die from it, your mind starts disassociating from your diseased body and laying blame on it. Regarding the body as the enemy, the mind knows it can no longer trust its body to sustain life. It takes only a short while for your body to catch up and fulfill this prophesy in the face of such gruesome expectations. Intervention at this point has to be aimed at resolving the misunderstanding between these warring parts of the self, to bring them together in a spirit of trust and renewed vigor for healing.

In later chapters I will talk about survival, because that is so important to all of us. But as the first step in healing yourself, let's take a few minutes to live in what may be the first moment of total freedom you have ever experienced from your ordinary life in order to reflect on what you are going to learn from freedom that will turn around the rest of your life, and will allow you to regain confidence and respect for your body. Let's use the horrible fact of your illness to jump-start growth and regain your integrity of self. I love being with people who have been told they are gravely ill. If they have gone through the process I will take you on in this book, they are the best adjusted and most lovingly spirited people on earth.

Not everyone uses illness productively in this way. So many folks I have worked with just want to get it behind them and go on as before - cut, burn, or poison the part of the body that is troublesome and without another thought, keep traveling along their same path.

Marti

Marti, age 48, was diagnosed a few years ago with a form of breast cancer that is so common we call it "garden variety." Because she had one positive node, she decided on a modified radical mastectomy and chemotherapy. She told me, "I just wanted rid of my breast as fast as possible. If my breast is my problem, I don't need it. Take it off. I don't want to dwell on this. I just want all this behind me. I want to forget about it." And forget, she did, for awhile, as she resumed her old life without a beat. Two years after completing her treatment, and putting it behind her, she discovered a recurrence in the other breast, and had to have a second mastectomy and more chemotherapy. I felt that if she did not take charge of this, there finally would be nothing left of her to cut.

Barbara

Barbara, age 53 was in a support group for breast cancer patients where they passed around a short survivor's guide I wrote that discussed very briefly such things as imaging, thriving, growing with illness, and nutrition. She was an executive in a pharmaceutical company. She had just been told that she had a very severe metastasis to the lymph nodes under her arm and was still in the staging process that would tell her if it had spread anywhere else. She read my material and then took the information home to Jack, her husband who also read it and said, "This is good information for both of us. Let's try it." Barbara and Jack slowly began to let go of some of the stressful and unrewarding aspects of their lives. They improved their nutrition. They started taking a Yoga class and learning to meditate. With the new friends they met in these classes, they learned to laugh again. Barbara told me the other day that having cancer was the best thing that had ever happened to her. She said,

> You know, I was existing before. We were both working long hours, coming home exhausted, and eating junk in the evening because nobody had the time or will to cook. We were both 20 to 30 lbs. overweight. We did a lot of heavy duty drinking in the evening to unwind. We exercised from January 2 to January 31, because that is as long as the New Year's resolutions lasted.

> One morning, just before my diagnosis, I looked in the mirror. I was appalled at my tired, lined face and thin hair. For the first time in years I allowed myself to take in the fact of my bloated face and body. I was totally shocked at how old-looking I suddenly appeared. I felt used up and profoundly alienated from everything around me. I asked myself, "Is this all there is to life?" I tried to remember when the last time was that I really, deep down, enjoyed something. Now I really feel spiritual about life. My life has a purpose and a meaning. I am healthier than I was at 30, and I look better than I did then. If this is cancer, bring on cancer!

The moment when you are told that you have a life-threatening illness, you will never feel more alienated or separated from everything and everyone you know and love as you do in that instant. This is the freedom that the great psychologist, Eric Fromm wrote about in his book, *Escape From Freedom*. Total freedom is a complete separation from all that surrounds us - a difficult, anxious, and unfamiliar state of being. But Fromm taught that allowing absolute freedom into our lives may be the only way we can grow as human beings. Otherwise, we are running, escaping, avoiding, and distancing ourselves from ourselves. The state of being alone inside ourselves is so very frightful that we have culturally approved ways of escaping from it. Dwelling in the pure unattached state of our humanness, without resorting to outside attachments and time-filling activity, is one of the scariest things one can imagine.

Barbara and Jack exemplified one way that most of us escape from freedom. We keep ourselves totally engaged in activities like work -busy, busy, busy. And when we are not working we are always doing something, planning something, remembering something, reading something. We talk incessantly on the cell phone. We watch endless television. Silence is not permitted.

I know for a fact that the purpose of my own busy activities is escape, resisting, being alone with myself. Complete freedom, to those of us who have had no opportunity to learn to use it productively, is akin to insanity. Instead, we seek ways to fill in the blank spaces with something – music, activities, drugs, mindless chatter - anything besides being with ourselves alone, and having to get to know what is going on inside.

No wonder we never had a minute's preparation for the freedom we now are experiencing; the freedom that intrudes with its unwelcome news that we may soon be radically free from all obligations and all relationships that we have so carefully tended and cultivated over the years. Placed among those who are seriously ill, we are set apart from our healthy living friends and family. Relegated to join the ranks of those who will soon be tossed out on our ears, we suffer with the idea that everyone else in the world, we suspect, will go on quite nicely without us, after a short period of grief, of course. Next year there won't even be flowers on my grave, we whimper, pitifully. We have never felt so alone, so remote, so bereft, so frightened.

In moments after a life-threatening diagnosis we are allowed to understand that there is no real escape. Your diagnosis has given you a vision of a future that puts you on a greased slide to a vast unknown, a departure from all your psychological comforts. To writers of dictionaries, freedom is not something in itself, but rather an absence of something - an absence of constraint, an absence of whatever binds, confines, oppresses, and entangles us. Stop and think about it. These things that bind, confine, oppress, and entangle us are what we call our lives. When we have a diagnosis that separates us from the ties that bind, we have literally lost our lives. In the song, *Me and Bobbie McGee,* Kris Kristofferson writes, "Freedom is another word for nothing left to lose." But it is in losing everything that you are forced into a discovery process in which you learn that there is another way to deal with freedom that surpasses mindless, compulsive behavior. This route, one that you may never have noticed before, promotes growth as you begin to understand in the deep way that you need to learn it, that no matter how cut off you feel, you are never an isolated self, but are always connected profoundly to everything and everyone. This realization leads to spirituality, which I will talk about in Chapter 9.

Viktor Frankl

The late psychiatrist and writer, Viktor Frankl lost his entire family in the German concentration camps. In his book, *Man's Search for Meaning* he described the most ghastly and dreadful things one can imagine. He had every reason to think he would die. He was starved of food and water, tortured, worked until he was exhausted, and more than anything, dehumanized. He and his companions were so thin they were unrecognizable. Their filthy skin was covered with bleeding sores and brutal bruises. They labored on because they knew that if they could no longer work, they would be immediately singled out in the morning inspection and placed among those sentenced to die. But after he was rescued, Dr. Frankl wrote a book about the most important thing that he learned - that beyond doubt, when everything is seized at once, what remains is human freedom. Freedom really is nothing left to lose. But Frankl concluded that it was this very freedom, and the suffering that followed that allowed him to pursue an understanding of the purpose and meaning of his life and to achieve spiritual growth.

Those of us who are diagnosed with a serious illness have learned how truly frightful, annihilating, immobilizing, and dehumanizing freedom is at first, as we live under the threat of death, and the immediate danger of losing everything we know. But listen to David's story of how he transformed freedom into becoming connected with others in a way that he never dreamed possible.

David

David was a carpenter who was diagnosed with AIDS in 1990, and learned that he was in the late stages. His t-cell count upon diagnosis was zero. He felt that his whole life along with everything he had always known was snatched away with one giant slash. He told me that all he could think of, day and night was, "I'm dead. I'm dead. That's it. Couple of months and I will be dead." This carpenter, who had no background or experience for leadership, used his freedom to reinvent himself. He went on to establish and lead two organizations for support and care of persons with HIV. Although only expected to live a few more months, David lived for 7 more years. At the end of his life, he told me that he never regretted having AIDS. Had he not, he would never have been given the incredible chance he had to learn about his purpose on earth and make a difference in his own and other's lives.

So now, I invite you to become part of this book, to learn how the vast freedom that now contains only the ghosts of remembered liaisons can be rebuilt and transformed into living. I invite you to use the chapters in this book to let me help you to surrender to this freedom in order to become a person with a life of meaning.

THE
FIRST
CHALLENGE:

Preparing Yourself Mentally
For Surviving And Thriving

Surviving starts out as a state of mind and a state of mental and physical readiness to live life to the fullest – no holds barred. The four chapters in this section help you to gain the hope, calmness, and courage that are forerunners of surviving and thriving after your diagnosis. You will learn in this section what kind of person you will become when you seek to be a survivor, what surviving is all about, and how to get ready emotionally to use all the information that this book has to offer you on surviving.

Chapter 1

Meet A Survivor: Me

Learning that I had a near zero chance of living another five years shook me to the core. I realized for the first time, that death is beyond doubt, an event that applies to me. Before it always had been what happened to someone else, preferably my distant neighbor's old grandparents. For more than a year after that, I lived in constant fear of a metastasis of my cancer, a fear that became almost unbearable every time I visited my oncologist and waited for the results of the tests that I was sure would put the seal on my appalling fate.

In April, 1983, I was a healthy person who only needed a routine physical exam. So I was stunned to learn that a virulent form of breast cancer had been living inside me for a long time. After interminable tests and a drawn out period of horrific waiting, I discovered that cancer had already invaded 7 out of 12 nodes under my left arm. I was in the peak of a life that was apparently defunct. Since I was the chair of a large department at The University of California, San Francisco, where I was also going for my care, the doctors and nurses treated me like a colleague, and that was not good. They gave me professional material to read that other patients would not have been exposed to. When looking over their material, I had the misfortune of running across the ghastly medical prediction that my five year prognosis was less than 5%.

In a panic, I hunted down as much information as I could find in my knowledge-rich medical center environment. I collared everyone I met to get their learned estimation of my chances with this or that treatment.

Everyone had an opinion. Listening expectantly, raising up my face up to theirs in anticipation of a forthcoming solution that would end this nightmare, I trusted everyone, and then after awhile, no one. I finally realized that the pronouncements that sounded so imposing all amounted to the same thing – take whatever they are willing to throw at you and try to hope for the best. So I chose to have 5 weeks of radiation and a year of a mixture of chemotherapy drugs.

Humans are protected from remembering the complete force of most of the strong emotions we have experienced in the past, so a lot of the raw fear, created by that unwanted bit of news, has been forgotten, and thank God for that. What I remember most clearly was when the nurse practitioner told me that there was a suspicious lump. I did not even know the awful truth of how bad it was. Still the physical impact of her diagnosis felt like a blow in my chest. I had difficulty getting my breath, and I became so light-headed that I was forced to sit down so I would not pass out. In some ways we never forget how we felt, although the impact is lessened over time. The thing that I know for sure is that no matter what happens to me now, I will never be that scared again in my whole life. I think about crashing in my car, being shot by a random bullet, spiraling toward the ground in a plane crash. Yes, I would be terrified, but my experience with getting beyond that first few months of my cancer diagnosis has left me with the confidence that I could endure anything that comes along, no matter how appalling, with more assurance than would have been possible before the diagnosis.

Those who have never been threatened in this way need to know what all of us go through who, without warning are summarily placed in the category of "soon dead." Closing my eyes in meditation this morning, I began to remember some of it but with many of the raw emotions missing. It helps me in my recollection to remember that I have heard the same, exact stories from innumerable men and women with cancer, HIV, and other serious diseases with whom I have worked, and these are continual reminders of a time in which cold dread horror and mindless panic had their hold on me for awhile.

Between bouts of panic, I remember feeling dead - hollow and empty, as though I were totally cleaned out inside, nothing of the slightest substance left. All my years of living, meant nothing to me because the emotions that had been connected to activities and people I knew and loved were too far out of reach. I imagined my friends going on living without me there. I was dazed and totally detached, yet I was able to do normal tasks such as driving, and working. Fortunately, for the first few months, I did not have to report to work everyday, because I was on a 4 month sabbatical. I was writing a book, which amazingly, I finished while struggling with all my angst and anxiety. Looking back, I think that it was a miracle that I could focus that much and I also realize that writing returned me to a reality that I could control and deal with.

I would wake up in the middle of the night in a cold sweat, shaking and scared. At times panic was almost a friend, a welcome relief from the vacuity of emptiness and dullness inside. I could not enjoy anything that had been dear to me in the past. I crawled though those early days in despair, not eating, sleeping, resting, playing, or living. I endured from doctor's appointment to doctor's appointment, hoping, wishing, and praying to hear some better news from all the scans and tests. I never did. My fate was settled in the hands of the tests and the rendering of bad news about my prognosis.

Listening to music made me more anxious. I could not sit though a movie or read a book. Alone, fears of what would happen to me were overwhelming, but in the presence of my non-diagnosed friends, I felt one down, defeated, pitied. And God knows, they could not pity me or write me off more than I did myself. I wanted their understanding, but not their charity or sympathy. I would try to pull myself together so I would not look like a "cancer patient," or someone who was dying, or someone who qualified as an object of concern or compassion. I would note their insouciance, their disregard for the final reality of their own lives - their insistence on seeing me as dying, but in denial about their own eventual mortality. I wondered how anyone could be happy. Forgetting that I used to be just like them, I thought, "Why are you laughing, trying to get ahead, make money, achieve fame, whatever? We are all going to die. Don't you know that, you idiots?"

During this period, some friends and colleagues would not look me in the eye. A couple of friends stopped calling altogether. I was so busy worrying about my loss of friends and taking care of other people's reactions to me that it was costing me precious energy. I hated to go in for scans and treatments. Not only did I resent having to acknowledge my cancer and participate in what I saw, given my prognosis, as the useless sham of my treatments. I remember thinking that my horrible prognosis must be the reason why so many of my caregivers had such funereal expressions on their faces when I walked into their clinics and offices. Even my surgeon did not come into the room to talk with me when he told me the wretched news about his examination of my lymph nodes. He stood in the doorway. When I started crying, he said in a whinny tone of voice, "Well, this is hard for me, too, you know." I was so angry that I never spoke to him again after that, and sought out another doctor to give me care.

Anger definitely served a good purpose for me. It relieved my depression and filled the gaping hole inside. Unrelenting anger, which I have found to be so typical of persons in the early stage of diagnosis, serves the valuable purpose of moving us along in doing something positive about our depressed state of mind.

Don't get me wrong, we patients often have a lot to be angry about. Systematically the "soon dead" are separated psychologically from the living, whom I call the "not-diagnosed-yet." Medical personal pity us, but keep us at a distance emotionally. Not a single one ever asked me how I was handling all this. Sometimes they tried to joke around a bit in a friendly way, but mostly they ignored me - looked through me or talked over me. I thought, "Maybe to them, I am already dead, so why should they get involved or care about me?" Or possibly I have only scared them; reminded them of their own death. I knew what my chances were from reading books, but I could also have read it in their faces. Nobody should know such a grim statistic about themselves. Nobody should be the recipient of care in which the caregivers show so clearly that they don't care, and are so obviously ready to move on to the patient in the next room who might be more curable.

This whole business of prognosis began to influence my thinking profoundly, and I allowed it to drain me emotionally and psychologically in the deepest ways. I leaned toward quitting my job in an irrational attempt to crash and burn my life. Fortunately, I was too immobilized to carry out my professional suicide intent. Shaking in my boots, I started reasoning: I will not see age 50; I will never see the year 2000; I am dead and gone. As I worked though counting the many things I would never again see, I began, very gradually to detect a glimmer of light somewhere inside. Almost imperceptibly, something positive was trying to force itself to the surface. It kept pushing at my mind in odd moments, long before I could apprehend its presence fully. Maybe that is why I decided to start walking, even though I was exhausted all the time. I started with a 20 minute walk at a slow pace.

In San Francisco, I lived a few blocks from a city called Colma, which has more cemeteries per square mile than any other city in the US. In Colma, there are far more dead people than alive. On my walk, I could not avoid passing one of the largest graveyards every time I left the house, and I would always avert my eyes, and run by it quickly. I don't know what the impetus was that turned this around, but one day instead of slinking by, I slowed down and stared at the cemetery. I did not know what I was going to do until I did it. In front of a number of astonished onlookers, I stood at the gate and shouted, "You will not get me yet!" WOW, that made me feel better. You can't imagine. I had looked IT in the face and defied it. I can't tell you how fantastic that felt. That was the day that my life would begin to turn around.

What I went though is a universal experience, indistinguishable from what countless other patients have told me in tearful accounts of their distress; descriptive of the lives of newly diagnosed patients in our health care system, a system that can deal with neither life nor death. If you have an illness like cancer or AIDS that is judged as a very serious illness, you know the agony of having caregivers withdraw, no longer able to treat you as an equal. You know how they talk to your family, not you. You know the anxiety of waiting for test results over a long weekend when the lab is closed, of not getting the facts to make good decisions, and finally, sorting out contradictory opinions from learned health practitioners. Worse, you understand how it feels to live through the unbelievable reality that this is happening to you. Your entire life can now be divided into two parts: before and after the diagnosis.

A few minutes ago, you were walking around like everyone else, breathing the air, griping about minute problems, wasting precious time, and now you are told that your life is finished. How did it happen that it was all over so fast? Anyone who has not been there cannot possibly understand entirely how you feel, although the best of them make your life easier by sticking by you and trying to understand. The lowest of them run like the craven cowards that they are. Your diagnosis really separates the sheep from the goats.

Several nice things came into my life that helped me along the road my mind was already trying to take me. My oncologist was one of the kindest and most caring of men. Too often he treated me like a colleague, so his message about my prognosis was realistically dim. He said that the best he could do was give me two more years of life for my one year of chemotherapy. That was horribly distressing. But he also went along with my ventures into the alternative world. He never made fun of them, and he supported me in reaching out for other forms of care. The nurse, who drew my blood every week, was very kind and hopeful for me as well. This is so unlike a number of patients with whom I have worked whose physicians belittled their efforts at self care; who implied or threatened that the person would have to seek care elsewhere if they got into these weird things; and who blatantly said that they were wasting their time and money by taking vitamins or by going to an acupuncturist or another kind of healer. My doctor also recommended a book by a radiation oncologist, Carl Simonton called, *Getting Well Again*. This small book contained the very useful information that started me on imaging my disease into remission, a topic that I discuss in detail in Chapter 7.

When my anxiety was still very high, Tom, one of my colleagues took me by the hand one day and said, "You have to take care of yourself. What vitamins and herbs are you taking?" Tom had AIDS, and in 1983, nobody knew much about what AIDS was, even for sure, what caused it to spread. He had decided, like many persons with AIDS at that time and since then, to seek out alternative forms of care. I was taking no supplements because I never believed that I needed extra vitamins, and I knew nothing about any alternative sources of help. He guided me to a place on Parnassus Avenue in San Francisco called the Vitamin Express where a very kind and knowledgeable man took me into a counseling room and went over all his recommendations. Some sounded bizarre to me then, but guess what? I took everything they told me to.

This was the first I had ever heard of something called Antioxidants. I learned that Antioxidant vitamins and minerals were substances that attacked something called free-radicals, and that free radicals were largely responsible for diseases such as cancer. I devoured the limited amount of literature that was available 25 years ago, trying to find out more. The only real research available was from the Linus Pauling Institute. I learned that Linus Pauling with a Scottish physician, Cameron, had done a clinical trial in Scotland, using only patients whose prognosis was so poor that they were no longer being given active treatment for cancer. They had been made as comfortable as possible and were expected to die quickly. Cameron put these patients into a special ward and gave them massive doses of vitamin C. They were matched with patients who were similar in every respect, except that they did not get vitamin C. The results were impressive and overwhelmingly positive. A few of these patients with terminal cancer actually recovered and went home cancer free. The rest all lived 2 to 3 times longer than their matched controls. In every case of those receiving vitamin C, the quality of life indicators were significantly higher than those who got usual care. I will discuss all my nutritional recommendations in detail in Chapter 10, and some of you may want to just skip to that chapter now, so feel free to do so, as I consider this information vital to recovery. Needless to say, I started on large doses of vitamin C as well as other antioxidants.

As much as I respected my doctor, I never wanted to entrust my entire future to an oncologist. I decided to look far a field to see what I could do for myself. With little help from my friends in medicine and nursing, but with an enormous assist from community groups and other patients who had been struggling with cancer and HIV, I gradually learned the self-care regime that I describe in this book; a regimen that I continue to this day, and that I believe saved my life, calmed me down, and finally, pushed me toward a state of optimum health. Gradually, I began to seek out sources of information that helped me to shape my own care, but at first, I needed to be taken under someone's wing. I count as one of my survival tools the fact that I have never turned up my nose at anything offered to me. I have taken classes in acupuncture, therapeutic touch, Reiki, massage, shiatsu, meditation, imaging, and have even taken 3 courses on how to be a psychic. I did not always buy into everything that was said by all these practitioners, but everything I have investigated has opened doors in my mind and added a bit of knowledge here and there that now is summed up in my personal philosophy and health practices. I may owe my survival to the fact that since the beginning, I have never limited myself or my potential sources of knowledge by prejudging them and comparing them with the tenets of the sciences in which I was trained or the religion in which I was brought up.

After almost a year of treatment, I was offered a very good position in Austin, Texas that allowed me to get away from all well meaning people who had gone through my diagnosis and treatment, and often had to suppress their sad feelings about my survival when around me. Frankly I was amazed that someone would even offer me a job – an endowed professorship with tenure - given my prognosis. In 1983, when I went for the visit to the new school, I said to the Dean, "Do you know what you are getting? I have cancer in an advanced state. I may not live too much longer." She assured me that she knew this and still wanted me there for as long as I would live.

This woman's response made me feel great, and it reinforced what I learned would be for me, a vital lesson for surviving - entrust your friendship to people who are positive about you and your survival, but let go, without guilt, of people who want to hang crepe over you or who walk by you with eyes downcast, hoping they won't have to talk to you. My first experiences with negativity had occurred right after my diagnosis. In the parking lot at the hospital, I ran into a woman I knew who had a Master's degree in Oncology Nursing, who had already heard about my diagnosis. Not only what she said, but also the look in her eyes conveyed to me that she felt I was a hopeless case. During the conversation, she kept saying things like, "Oh, no. How terrible this is for you. What a dreadful prognosis." Her mind-set made me furious, and I avoided her after that. For days, I ranted about how professionals in oncology need to stop projecting their own fears of dying onto their patients. That was how I felt then. Now, I would be able to just look her in the eye and say gently, "This is very hard for me, but it is not terrible. It is another experience in my beautiful life. When you have a moment, I wonder if you would stop and try to consider it from my point of view. An important thing that you might consider when you put yourself in my place is to think about what my options are. I have the option to prepare grimly for the worst, or as you say, dwell on how terrible this is for me, or the option to face the challenge of every day that I live with hope, regardless of my health."

So it has gone for 20 years now; my transformation from victim to thriver. It would take many years before I moved fully from my panic about dying from cancer to embracing life in all its states of illness and health; and before the realization hit me in a way that I could hear it clearly, that no one knows how long anyone has to live. Reasoning this out, it means that nobody is dying more than anyone else. We are all living for as long as we live. Furthermore, the purpose of my life on this earth is to experience it fully as a human being. In all states of health, I am intended to go face to face with life until I die, not to sit around like a ghoul, waiting for the inevitable. It was years, too, and after a ton of experience in working with people in the final stages of life, that the truth finally sank in that my unavoidable destiny is as much a part of my life as anything else I do on earth. When my time comes, I will be on familiar terms with all the wisdom that I need, and I will confront my death with courage and a sanguine, cheerful spirit, secure in the knowledge that I will always be myself. It is most pathetic and pitiable when we waste our lives in worry about our death. When we really dig in and begin to enjoy living, fears of dying will take care of themselves. A major outcome of becoming a thriver has been the mounting insight, gained after the bleak news of my prognosis, that dying will not lessen me, diminish me, or destroy who I am. It will add to my human experience.

Chapter 2

What Is A Survivor?

Researchers and clinicians have identified a number of personal characteristics of people who have lived beyond their medical prognosis. Do not be discouraged if every one of these characteristics does not describe you. Look at them as survival pointers that can indicate new directions for garnering support, handling your illness, managing your care, and steering yourself into new ways of interpreting your illness.

Dealing with a serious illness uncovers the enormous amount of untapped strength that we have inside. It brings out the very best in each of us as we are challenged to reach deeply within to find new ways to confront a world that is falling apart. One of my patients said, "I have always held my mother up as such a strong person, and I still do. But in dealing with everything that is coming up now, I realize that I am strong, too." You might discover that after admiring someone else's courage for years, you suddenly find that you are just as strong and capable as the person you admire, and you will use this insight to hold up and admire the heroic person that is you.

Taking Responsibility And Taking Charge Of Your Care

Long term survivors accept the reality of their diagnosis, but refuse to perceive it as a death sentence, and after an initial period of shock, they get moving. But first, let me talk about what taking responsibility is not. Taking personal responsibility for your health does not mean that you feel guilty for anything that you might think you have done to cause your illness. Too many times we are encouraged to think that we, the victims, are guilty, while others, who are still healthy, are blameless and perfect people. Nothing is ever gained by taking this approach, and there is no evidence to support this separation of the ill from the well in the vast majority of cases. I have heard a lot of ridiculous stories of victim blaming. The mother of one of my students, who was gay, told her that being gay was why she developed diabetes. When a single mother developed breast cancer, someone told her that it was because God was telling her she should be married. When people ask you what you did to cause your illness, or tell you why they think you have it, don't take on their accusation as responsibility or guilt. Just let them know how thankful you are that since they live such a flawless life, they will end their lives in a hospital dying of nothing at all.

When taking personal responsibility, instead of becoming a door-mat, thus acting in a way that gives others the impression that they have a right to take over your decisions, you are assertive and yes, maybe angry about what is happening around you. You don't let other people push you into decisions that you are not ready for, nor do you let them tell you that they know everything that is good for you, and therefore, you should only listen to them. You may have to remind the people who care about you that they need to show it by joining you in seeking new information instead of trying to restrict you or intimidate you into adhering to their point of view.

So taking personal responsibility means that you remain in charge of your own life. You learn as much as you can about your illness and all the ways to begin healing. You do not assign blame for your illness to others or yourself. But a small caveat here - give yourself time to come to grips with your diagnosis before you dive in and start charging around like a deranged, aging explorer in a determined search for the fountain of youth. Almost al-ways, time is on your side, and you can move slowly into your explorations on health. While you rightly may feel that you want rid of your disease quickly, even yesterday, if possible, you can allow yourself adequate time to regroup before you hurry into action. As soon as you can, begin to locate sources of support and information that will allow you to take back your life.

Developing An Active Coping Style In Relation To Health

This characteristic is very much related to the first one. When I first started counseling persons with HIV disease and cancer I would think, "If we can just get this person's fear under control, we can get started." Slowly, I learned that the early panic and fear that I experienced myself and have seen in almost everyone with whom I have worked have an important place in healing. At first these emotions immobilize us, but as we work through them, they give us the drive to cope with whatever we are dealing with. Thinking back to Viktor Frankl's experience that I discussed in the *Introduction*, it is in suffering that we learn about who we are and of what we are capable. Suffering serves a definite purpose for growth and maturity.

Having suffered the worst fear and terror imaginable, you can begin to use your fear to your advantage, to employ patterns that psychologists call "active coping." If you were not afraid for your life, you would not be inclined to do very much problem-solving. Coping is fueled by your belief that you can influence your health outcome through your own efforts. I think this is one of the most important attributes of the long-term survivors with whom I have worked. Now I can almost spot a survivor in the first few minutes of conversation by observing the presence or absence of this distinguishing quality in the period after the shock has worn off, and when it is time to take charge. I see some people who stoically soldier on in an attempt to bury the trauma and get it all over with. They might say, "I'll just let my doctor take it out and consider myself cured;" or, "You do the research for me and tell me what vitamins to take and I will take them." Hearing this lack of interest in participating as an equal partner in one's healing concerns me very much. It is true that people have to be more passive at first, when what they know would not fill the hole in a nit's ear, but a life-long pattern of turning your fate over to any practitioner, while absolving yourself of the major responsibility for your own healing is not a good idea. No health provider has the unique knowledge of us that we have of ourselves; neither do they have the time and the interest to invest in you that you have for yourself. We are, if nothing else, the keepers of our own lives and our own health. We have been in charge of ourselves all our adult lives, as we make many small decisions everyday about relationships, spirituality, exercise, diet, and so on. Many small decisions have added up to diminish or enhance our total health picture. It is your accruing knowledge of what is good for you, your belief in your health routines, and the emerging elaboration of your personal philosophy that will now allow growth and survivorship.

Coming Up With A Reason To Live Beyond Fear Of Dying

Survivors have a commitment to life in terms of "unfinished business," unmet goals, or as yet unfulfilled experiences and wishes. They have a sense of meaningfulness and purpose in life and look forward to its unfolding. The first thing that happens when one receives a life-threatening diagnosis, is that meaning and purpose suddenly disappear as we try to imagine a world without us in it, creating despondency and depression. For all but a tiny few, this is only a temporary state. The most important force for fighting despondency is caring. Caring for and caring about involves reaching out. It

12

entails remembering whom we love and what we enjoy.

Ronald

Ronald, age 82, was in a sad state when I counseled him at the request of his daughter. He had suffered a series of strokes a few years before I met him. He was wheelchair bound and was sometimes incontinent. But he had been progressing slowly in his recovery until a few months before when his wife died rather suddenly. After she died his goal was to die too. He had regressed into a mild dementia, sitting alone in a chair and staring into space, neither talking nor acknowledging his daughter, except to rebuff her attempts to care for him. Ronald said he was happy before his wife died, but he now had no feeling at all for anything. I asked him to tell me what happiness had meant to him before. He answered that it was the companionship with his wife, the way they shared, gave to each other, and loved each other. After he told me this, I assured him that I did not see anything wrong with his wanting to join his wife, but I was very concerned about the way he was dying, leaving this earth in such a wretched state. I then said to him. "I have good news for you. If you want to die soon, you probably will. Still, I hate to see you die as such an unhappy and depressed man when you tell me that the happiness of sharing and mutual giving has been so important to you all your life. I wonder if there is some small thing that you could give to somebody now." He could not think of a thing. So I said, "Your daughter loves you and is very worried about you. She spends a lot of her time and energy every day trying to make you comfortable. I wonder if you could give to her now by telling her what this means to you?" He nodded reluctantly, so I called his daughter in, and asked her to sit in a chair facing Ronald. With a lot of help from me, he told her in a halting voice. "I know I am not easy to be with. Thank you for all you are doing for me." She started crying, and my eyes became moist as well. She held him in a hug for awhile, while she told him how important it was to have her father with her, because since her mother had passed away she felt very bereft. Then, I asked them to think together of one small thing they could give to each other every day, perhaps sharing a kind word or a remembrance of their late mother and wife. Ronald did die within a year, a victim of stroke, immobility, and to a great extent, still, loneliness. But he had started to eat again. He liked to have certain sections of the newspaper read for him, and he began to enjoy reviewing with his daughter the things about their past life that had always brought happiness to him. This experience allowed them to refocus on their caring for each other, and to progress beyond the worst of the grief. Ronald turned out to be a survivor for as long as his life went on.

13

Finding New Meaning As A Result Of The Illness

After a serious diagnosis, many people begin to feel the wake-up call that comes from the insight that life is not a dress rehearsal. Instead, our lives represent the sum total of time that we have to meet our goals and let our presence make a difference in the world. For so many of the people I knew in my work with the seriously ill, this meant resolving old hurts and foraging more positive relationships with friends and family who had parted ways because of physical distance, conflicts, or anger and resentment. It also involved finding meaning in new activities and relationships.

Helena

Helena was a former prostitute and addict who had contracted AIDS. Because she was in the final stages of the disease, and near death, she was admitted to a hospice for persons with AIDS. She had always born abusive relationships, and at the time of her admission to our hospice was totally alone. Under the loving care of the hospice workers and the other residents, Helena found herself in the middle of an intense circle of love and genuine attention for the first time in her life. Whereas before, she had been bitter and suspicious, she let down her guard and let others in. She blossomed. She recovered her health in fact, and instead of dying, was discharged. After discharge, in remission from her opportunistic diseases, Helena had a whole new grip on a satisfying life, and for the first time in her memory was able to give to others and receive love.

Many survivors, finally beginning to realize that life is not what happens while you are making other plans, started moving ahead in work-related goals instead of marking time. I know at least 6 men and women who are long term survivors of HIV, who started college or graduate school after their diagnosis. Most of their friends thought they were wasting their time and taking up a slot that a "healthy" person could have filled. Once you have a serious diagnosis, and are placed in the category of "soon dead," the outlets that all people need for continuing to have meaning in one's ordinary life are low on the priority list, in the opinion of those around you. You are supposed to start living a "saintly life" with a grand meaning - whatever that is - or dismally waiting for the grim reaper to flash his ugly smile in your face.

Survivors learn that most of life's meaning is contained in the engrossment of everyday experiences. This insight was summed up for me in an interview reported, in a *New York Times Magazine* that David Letterman had with the dying singer and song writer, Warren Zevon. Letterman asked him if he had learned anything from his illness about life and death. Zevon replied, "How much you are supposed to enjoy every sandwich."

Each one of the HIV survivors who went back to school and met the personal goal of attaining a college degree also seemed to be enjoying every sandwich. They took pride not only in the attainment of a degree, but also in the journey, the process of learning. Too, instead of knuckling under to submit to the humiliation of support from public assistance, they are proud of jobs in which they are producing and giving back to society. Even if they had not graduated, they all got encouragement from other survivors to meet their personal goals instead of cowering in a corner waiting to die.

James

I met James when I went to an HIV support group to lead a discussion on thriving and surviving. Instead, James taught me some things about thriving. James was a teacher, but he had always wanted go to law school. After his diagnosis, he realized that he did not want to die without fulfilling this lifelong goal. Against the advice of his family, he pursued his dream to become a lawyer. Particularly at exam time, the pressures from his job and his law studies created a stress that was almost unmanageably high. His family urged him to quit. It often seemed to him that in their overprotection, they resented his efforts at self-improvement. He said, "I suppose they wanted me to sit on the front porch and rock until I die." James persisted anyway. He told me with some irony in his voice that two of his healthy law school classmates had died before graduating, one of a suicide and one of an abrupt cardiac event, while he, the "terminally ill" one graduated and passed the bar. At this point, another member of the support group chimed in, provoking laughter from the entire group, with the information that he had outlived the doctor who had told him a couple of years ago to "start getting his affairs in order."

In becoming a lawyer, James achieved precisely the same thing as many of his healthy classmates, the realization of a life's dream. Over the next few years, while James worked as an attorney in HIV organizations representing persons with AIDS, helping them with wills and other legal issues, he battled his own demons of recurring opportunistic infections. All the same, he rarely missed a day of work. His legal work made him feel complete, like a whole person, in a way that he had not experienced before. Nothing we can accomplish in life is more meaningful than work that meets our own needs for fulfillment while helping others. Had James not had HIV, I suspect that he would not have had the drive to pursue his dream – he would have kept putting it off for another day until finally, there were no more days. And, of course, the subsequent meaning for living that he found would have been missing forever from his life.

Finding New Ways To Become Physically Healthy

A serious illness provides a wake up call about health practices. Before our illness most of us knew very well that there are a number of things we could do to improve our heath, but being the humans we are, we tend to make excuses or put off doing those positive things that affect the way we feel every day. For most of the people with whom I have worked, the new choices and regimens they have adopted after their diagnosis have made them healthier than they were before the diagnosis.

A very limited perspective is looking at health as only the absence of disease. A state of health also prevents disease and helps us recover quickly from diseases that we do acquire. But much more than that, health is an affirming state of being that gives rise to exuberance. Health lets us enjoy the promise that each day holds for our explorations into a life that rewards with happiness and feelings of satisfaction. In health, we wake up from a sound sleep feeling refreshed and eager to get started on our choice of daily activities. Health provides the energy and the verve for a successful life. In finding ways to survive, we automatically learn about health because the same things that affect health also cure disease.

In Part Three of this book, I describe the activities and choices that I recommend for improving physical health. But so much of this information can be found scattered in sources that we all know about because we run across them every day in the daily newspapers, popular magazines and television.

Albert and Cliff

Albert was an accountant whom I met while doing HIV work in a peer-run clinic that Albert had founded. He was in his middle 40s, and his partner, Cliff was 10 years younger. Through their clinic, they counseled others on prevention of HIV. Early in our relationship, they invited me to dinner. After sipping on tomato juice instead of a cocktail, I was served a fantastically tasty meal of home-made pasta with fresh vegetables, garlic, onions, and tofu, and a to-die-for desert made with fresh fruit. Having once been heavy drinkers, they no longer drank alcohol except for very special occasions. Both were studying Yoga and meditation. Both were receiving acupuncture weekly. They proudly showed me photographs going back 10 years that showed how much younger they look now than before. In his 20s, Cliff had looked dissipated. He had been a junk food eater, a heavy drinker, and had used injecting drugs, as well. Now, well-nourished, clean and sober, his large brilliant blue eyes, surrounded by a clear, alabaster sclera, were stunning. His skin was clean and moist; his hair healthy looking and abundant. If I judged just by his appearance, I would have to say, that he was the healthiest person I have ever seen. What was so impressive was the excitement they now got out of life every day, the happiness ensuing from work with their peers, the energy that they brought to everything they did, and how much they looked forward to enjoying every second of their life.

Most of the time when people start a new health practice, like exercise or changes in their diet, they do not stay on them long enough to really feel them making a difference, and so after a few weeks of starving for the foods on their accustomed diets, and the aching, racking muscle and joint pain from exercise, they give up completely. But after a serious diagnosis, going back to the old ways of doing things is not an option for most people if they want to continue to live. As a result they stay on the new practices long enough to feel the full effects and learn to enjoy the results of the new patterns on how they feel. So what all of us survivors, like me and like Albert and Cliff have discovered, is that the way we feel when we are healthy is what spurs us on to search out ways to be ever more healthy. The wish to get well got us started, and the way we now experience life as healthy people keeps us going in the new grove.

Becoming Involved With Others With The Same Diagnosis

When I went for my radiation treatments, I waited for my technician in the women's waiting room, sometimes for up to an hour. There I met dozens of women with cancer. Nobody was shy about socializing. Here we were, horrible, ghettoized cancer patients, each looking worst than the last, but each hopeful about our progress, and each willing to share any information that we were coming up with that would help the others. Lila, who had advanced lung cancer, and who was only expected to live for a few more months, was a technical writer who had access to a lot of alternative information. She brought in numerous articles on antioxidants. We gave each other emotional support, grieving when things got worse, cheering when the outlook was improved. Another thing that hit me, just in looking around, was that there were other people who were worse off than I was. I had been feeling so sorry for myself until I met a woman with end of life cancer, who was on portable oxygen, lying on a stretcher, and could not take a whole breath without severe coughing. After noting what she was dealing with, I found it harder to justify my "poor me" attitude. Everyone, not just me, had their demons, their fears, and their worries. Listening to their stories and sharing my own brought on the feeling that we were all in the same boat. At times it did not matter whether or not the boat was sinking. What resonated comfort was the huddled warmth of comradeship among those suffering from a terrible, devastating disease.

Formal support groups that are organized for people to share and receive support and information are a God-send for many people. They are usually full of real encouragement. But be warned that there are support groups that are supportive, and there are those that are not supportive. One man who was newly diagnosed with colon cancer, said that in the group he attended, everyone was sitting around waiting to die, so he left and never tried another support group. Ronda, trying to access information that would aid her to deal with breast cancer found that there are support groups that limit access to alternative information, and outright ban group members bringing in or recommending outside material that may be different from the material the organization hands out. She is one of several women who have told me that in this nationally recognized support group for cancer, someone had tried to hand out copies of my *Survivor's Guide* in the group, and got told that they did not allow information describing alternative forms of care to be distributed. She managed to secure a copy of my guide anyway, and seeing that it contained my email address, wrote to thank me, and she also told me what happened. My advice to her and to you is to avoid people and groups who limit your explorations to their own single point of view.

The Final Lesson: Keep Tuned

It may appear that I have boiled down survivorship to only the seven points that are listed above, but nothing is ever quite this simple. You will be able to identify some of your other characteristics that will help you learn how to survive. If you are confused about how to get started in becoming a survivor, take heart. All the rest of this book is devoted to elaborating and providing the detail and strategies needed for pinpointing and honing your characteristics for survival.

Chapter 3

Dealing With The Emotional Responses
To A Threat To Health

Vulnerability, helplessness, loss, and fear of the unknown create severe emotional reactions to illness. These feelings are further compounded when the usual skills of problem solving that we have used all our lives seem to be ineffectual to tackle the problems that loom over like a storm cloud at a picnic. Yesterday you were involved in what you used to call your life. Today, dreams for the future seem to be in ruin, and as you struggle to recover your life, you find yourself blocked at every turn by an entirely unknown phenomenon that has a stranglehold on your thoughts and feelings, day and night. Who would not be incredibly upset and horrified?

A loss of one's health produces inconceivable fear and stress, followed by mourning for what was. Then the frustration of dealing with an unknown illness and confronting caregivers who at times do not seem to really care or appear to even know what they are doing, leads to anger, the likes of which you have never come across in yourself before. And if you are not angry, it is probably because you are too depressed to feel much of any emotion at all except sadness. In this chapter I will pull apart the meaning of these emotions in an effort help you to understand what these feelings mean and what you can do to move yourself through them in a way that creates health. These emotions have both positive and negative effects on your ability to heal and to cope with your illness and treatment. It is important to sort out which is which so that you can move through the negativity, while resolving the grief in a way that will increase your ability to gain control over what is happening. The feelings that are driving you down at first may actually be helping you to begin your journey toward health.

The Process Of Grieving

Shock, fear, and stress are the first reactions to deteriorations in health. This gradually abates, believe it or not. It really does. But when it does, you are not finished with working though your emotions. At this point, most people enter into the stages of grief that have been identified as mourning, anger, and finally resolution. These stages are not step-wise, so for much of our lives we go back and forth among them, as we confront the multiple losses that are products of being on earth. As we learn to live with a particular loss over time, the duration of the negative emotions will usually become shorter and shorter until finally, the suffering they cause is experienced as only a brief reaction before the calm again sets in again. Even resolution of loss does not protect you forever from recurring episodes of fear, mourning, and anger that may crop up at odd times. You can use this progression of emotions to open the way toward an understanding of health and living. You can initiate a process of discovery that takes you deeper and ever deeper into a journey that reveals the countless ways of improving your health and increasing your human potential. This same process will support you as you venture down strange, but wonderful paths that are far a field from where you set out.

Before, nose to the grindstone, you may have marched in rote fashion through your precious life, never taking enough time to stop and meditate on what wonderful promises life may hold for you. This is a state that the writer, Thomas Moore, called "loss of soul," an epidemic in our hurried, competitive culture. But now, having to confront your very life, you will develop a bird's eye view by stepping far enough away from your routines to see that possibilities abound. Like Moore, I do not believe that in order to care for our souls, we have to transcend the persons we once were. And like Moore, I believe that the formula for good living comes out of accepting ourselves in our non-perfect human state, while dealing with everyday problems with as much dignity and grace as is possible at the moment. Moore calls this course of action "fostering soulfulness in our every day lives." As we struggle to understand this lesson, we discover that the grand meaning of our lives is only what we do every day with regard to the love and respect that we hold for ourselves and others. I will go into this more in the next chapter when I talk about how to become a thriver. Suffice to say here, having an opportunity to discover more of the soul while living ordinary lives is why so many patients with whom I have worked have told me that it was worth being smacked over the head with a serious disease. Too, this growing insight is what seems to segregate us at times from the persons we once thought we were and the lives we once led. As we look around and see others acting like we have always acted – living life with such determined grimness and lack of joy - we will at first feel seriously separated and filled with the trepidation that accompanies those on the less traveled road. Living through your early emotions is a wretched experience, and so that is the main issue that I will discuss here, because we need to get them behind us, while extracting the most we can from living through them.

Fear And Stress

Fear and stress are the most typical first reactions to the shocking news that your health may be in trouble. Difficult as they are, the very fact that they almost always accompany bad news about health means that they are part of the normal human protective response. When something is normal for human beings, we know that there is a reason for its existence. Human beings, like all creatures on this earth are programmed to protect life. Hans Selye, the leading stress researcher wrote that the presence of stress means that there is something out there to be feared or that we believe should be feared, and the stress is calling attention to it so that we can adjust what we are now doing. So stress is a healthy mechanism that calls forth an adaptive response to whatever is endangering life, and this reaction allows one to learn skills that promote good coping ability. Fear for our lives, as miserable as it is, keeps us from taking unnecessary risks. It warns us from danger. More positively, it sends the message that we need to get moving, confronting whatever is threatening us.

At first, fear will no doubt immobilize you, but this is a temporary condition that lasts until your body and mind have a chance to adjust to changing views of yourself and changes in needed life skills to cope with your illness. Fear will decrease as you gain the knowledge you need to identify your options, and when you mobilize your support for coping and decision making.

Donald

Donald is a 36 year old man who has known about his HIV diagnosis for 8 years. This is what he said when I talked to him about how he was living with his diagnosis.

I thought I had my fear well in hand. My spirituality has been growing by leaps and bounds. I had begun to feel that I was being rocked in God's comfortable hands and that I understood that the reason that I was put here on earth was to grow and to help other people. I thought nothing could scare me anymore. Then last week I went to the doctor and found that my t-cell count had dropped again to an all time low. I totally freaked. I did not expect that reaction. I thought I was beyond being panicked about all this. Then I did what I have been taught to do in my support group and in my meditations – I looked at what the fear was telling me.

Donald's response to a threat to his body is the normal fight or flight reaction. His fear of bodily harm does not mean that his spirituality is failing him. Instead, his terror corresponds exactly to what he is supposed to feel when his body is in danger. In this case, fear helped Donald come to the realization that he had been taking the respite from his HIV symptoms for granted, and that he had been pushing himself at work beyond what was healthy for him. He saw that he needed again to pay attention to his body's needs for good food, rest, exercise, and relaxation. Because HIV is a disease with many ups and downs, Donald has been through this many times before, and he is learning to look behind the fear for what it is trying to tell him about his body or his soul. He also knows that each time he is scared he will attend to it in a way that gets him beyond it quickly. Fear that accompanies potential harm is what gives all living beings their first line of defense for preservation of life. But fear does not need to rule our lives. Not to have the capacity to ameliorate it would erase fear's effect as a positive response to danger. Fear alerts us to danger that is out there, and then steps into the background while we move into other normal processes that are constructive to mental and spiritual health.

Mourning And Depression

Getting out of depression is of vital importance, since it has such a devastating effect on the immune system and thwarts the will to live. But the mourning that follows loss of health is normal, and cannot or should not be rushed. It helps to know that there is an endpoint to the terrible feeling of flatness and despair. It is important not to treat medically this normal phase of grief. Mourning follows any significant loss, and it helps us to deal with the loss whether it is loss of a marriage, a close family member or friend's death, or loss of health. Mourning follows loss because it helps us deal with

22

the enormity of the loss and the accompanying emotions - feeling bereft, numb, tearful, defenseless, and hopeless. When someone close to us dies, we simply do not step over the dead body and go on with our lives. Similarly when we lose aspects of our health, we do not just say, "Well, there goes my health, let's see what else I can focus on." In the process of grieving for your loss of health, you say goodbye to the old person you were in proper fashion before you endeavor to see how you can make lemonade from any of those annoying lemons that have been cast into your lap.

Occasionally the mourning period turns into a depression that needs to be treated medically. If it lasts in a way that significantly interferes with living for more than around 6 to 8 weeks, professional help may be in order. This professional support may be in the form of personal or family counseling or perhaps asking for a prescription for a mild anti-depressant. Most times, though, self-help is the best remedy. The best self help advice I can offer you is to go back to what you have always done – return to doing the things that have always given you satisfaction, and do what you are best at doing. Until you get through the mourning period you cannot address your growth potential, or become the person you always dreamed you would be, or deal with any other aspects of thriving with illness. Take one step at a time.

Anger

My mourning period was characterized by a feeling of emptiness. I could not enjoy any of the things that had been so dear to me all my life, including reading or sitting outside enjoying the wind on my face. The first emotion that I experienced after the emptiness was anger, and it felt good – a relief from the void. I described in the introduction how angry I was at one of my doctors, the surgeon because he not only practically shouted his findings to me while standing at the door to my room, he complained that this was hard on him, too when I started crying. I practically became irrational every time I talked about him. "Hard on him," I would scream. "Somebody needs to tell him how to be a doctor." But in truth, the anger, as painful as it was, reminded me that I could still feel something, and I assure you that feeling anything is far better than feeling nothing.

Like mourning, anger is helpful to move the grief process along a little farther. I have met very few people who were not angry at something or someone after a serious diagnosis. This anger is not always due to an internal response. When dealing with the sluggish, and at times, inadequate health care system, people have a lot to be legitimately angry about. But, anger is also the emotion that bothers people when trying to carry out rational business with those providing care. Many ill people find themselves inexplicably angry at doctors, nurses, technicians and others who are providing treatment, especially when they are kept waiting or when they feel that they are not getting the attention they deserve. Smoldering over unintended slights, their reaction becomes dysfunctional when they become so emotional that they cannot engage their caregivers in the type of assertive conversation that results in getting one's way. Nevertheless over the course of working with a number of survivors, I have learned to see most angry responses as a sign of strength; as a coping response that augurs well for one's ability to fight illness.

But anger can also take over the whole life of the person and act as a barrier to good communication. So use your anger for the good, but begin your work to get it the worst of it behind you. How we do this is individual. There is so much to be angry about because even in the best of care facilities you will, at times, experience an almost total loss of control, endless waiting, ambiguity, and bad news. The best adjusted patients seem to get angry, but then can turn it around, after the crisis has passed, into a funny tale that sends fellow patients who are in the same boat into gales of laughter. I got a great response when I mimicked my surgeon's self-absorption and unprofessional manner of telling me that I was going to die soon. This rerouted my anger into a source of support, comfort, and camaraderie. Working through my anger, I gradually stopped taking it personally, and was able to bring to a close my way of seeing this doctor as a mean man who was out to ruin my parade. I started to see him as another human being, really just another flawed human being like me - granted he had an appalling bedside manner, and he could not be there for me. But like all human beings, he is munching his way through life, dealing with his own world and trying to do the best he can at the moment. I suppose it was hard on him.

The way to contend with all these fearsome emotions is by going back to some of your normal routines of living, becoming ever more aware, in a concrete way, of the special resources that you have used in the past to get beyond seemingly irresolvable problems. Many of your strengths can be found in your unique personality and your learned coping ability. Some of the most useful qualities are the willingness to try to see things in an optimistic light; to find many ways of making the best of an awful situation; to have perseverance when looking for solutions to seemingly unsolvable problems; to endeavor to open yourself up to all the sources of support and information that are around you; and finally, to be determined to use your illness to find as much as you can about your health and disease so that you can take charge of you.

Diane's Experience Changed Liz

Sometimes the most chance encounters can help us with the depression, anger, and self-pity that we feel when seriously ill. Liz told me that she learned an astonishing lesson about living when she was in the waiting room for radiation therapy for her lung cancer. She was hunched down in her chair in her backless gown, totally absorbed in feeling sorry for herself when Diane walked in, supported on the arm of her friend. Half of Diane's face and neck were eaten away by cancer. One eye was missing. She had to spit out her saliva into a Kleenex because she could not swallow. She had no voice. Diane's physical appearance and her wretched condition were so appalling that Liz turned away so that she would not have to look. But then Diane wrote something on a pad to her friend. Her friend told Liz, "Diane was just commenting on what a glorious day it is outside, and how thankful she is to be alive to see it." Liz, totally taken back at this display of living amidst suffering, realized that in her self absorption, she had not even been aware of what kind of day it was. Believe me, when she left the hospital that day, she took notice, and has never failed to do so since.

Chapter 4

Beyond Surviving: Preparing Yourself For Thriving

Thrivers are learning to live well. They find a way to articulate and feel comfortable about the purpose for which they are on earth. They appear to live longer, but they realize that a long life with an absence of meaning is not a goal worthy of their energy. Their hope, optimism, and spirituality help them to use the principles presented in this book to improve their overall health. After a period of adjustment, thrivers describe their lives as full and rich. What they have learned about living has allowed a presence to creep into their consciousness that informs meaning.

As a thriver, one of the most pressing lessons that you first confront upon finding out that you have a serious illness is how much you absolutely do not want to die. There is no space for death in any of your plans. Of course, no healthy person wants to die. The drive to preserve life is a sign of health. But living is far more than not dying. As a thriver, you will transform from a person who trudges through the days, asking, "Is this all there is for me?" into a flourishing person who chooses happiness on a daily basis.

Because your life has been threatened, you will be forced to acquire a personal understanding of death, and recognize the fact that death is a part of life that is just as normal as breathing. When I thought about this as it applied to me, I realized that my illness gave me the great insight to become a better person and a better nurse; to engage more fully in life; to counsel others about their need for nutrition and spiritual growth; to comfort friends and hospice residents when they were dying; to begin to uncover the meaning of health for me; and, finally, to write this book. I realized that the purpose of my life is to experience it, and that lying around moping about my illness was not getting on with this goal.

Facing the fact of death does not promote death. It upholds living, because you allow the whole purpose of your existence to unfold – and eventually you will evolve a deep understanding of why you are on earth at this particular time. Reconciling fears and developing a personal way of thinking about the meaning of life and death is a constructive task that thrivers engage in because they are involved in a fierce process of living that puts to right the apprehensions that are rampant in our culture that thwart living fully and dying with dignity. Now, the illness that has left you raw has also stripped from you the facade that may have blinded you to your authentic self. At first, this is unbelievably scary, but you will be guided in the next part of the book to ways that will allow you to emerge from the deep hole in which you have been hiding.

When I was first diagnosed, dying was the thing that I was the most terrified of. I have found that this is the case with almost everyone I have met with a serious or potentially terminal diagnosis. If you have not been through this terrible shock, it is hard to imagine. I believe that we accomplish the enormous feat of unraveling our fear largely though two ways: by living a thriving life, and through the reflective ways of healing that I present in the next part of this book, in which you learn that help lies within you and all around you. The rhythm of life becomes, living to the hilt, then reflecting; then living to the hilt in reflection. I challenge the notion, so often promulgated by the health care community, that ignoring the dire consequences of the diagnosis and engaging fully with life in the face of a serious illness produces "false hope." This discouraging message is so much a part of the ambient culture in which ill persons live. It inhibits all efforts at sustaining life, and masks all the opportunities that illness has shifted to within our close vision.

As you enter the pages of this book that present your next two challenges, and begin to apply them to yourself, I invite you to start on a path of learning about yourself and the meaning and purpose of your life that will help you continue to live with exuberance until the day you die. Having a serious illness in which you realize how precious life is, you begin to discover a quality of life previously not dreamed of. Almost nobody would wish a crisis of this proportion upon themselves in order to grow, so such attitudes are always held by those of us who are looking back on a negative experience. But thriving and surviving are two very different ways of going on with your life whether you have a serious illness or not. If all your life amounts to is, "tired of living, and feared of dying," then there is not too much point to it all.

There are things that you can do while you are still in crisis that will put you in the best position to absorb the information that I cover in the second and third challenges, and to set you on a road of thrivership. The *first* thing that most thrivers have to do before they begin the process of thriving is to identify and gather around them needed support for survival, including sorting out your relationships with the people who are important in your life. In doing this, you begin to learn the truth of what other people mean to you. If you are like most of us, you will find out who your friends are quickly. Rarely do other people, upon finding out that you are seriously ill, maintain the same degree of closeness they always had with you. Some are made distant - they run, physically or emotionally, in the opposite direction because of their own fear. Others become closer and more supportive, giving of their social and spiritual selves. Sorting out your support networks early can help save you from a lot of hurt and anger.

We have to find new ways of being with friends and family after a serious diagnosis because our energy is limited, and we are still working through our own emotions. I learned to avoid contact with the "Crepe Hangers," people who already have you in the grave – who want to bury you before you are dead. Later, I was gradually able to assess whom I wanted to let back in my life.

The *second* way that we prepare ourselves for learning to thrive is to strive to become true with ourselves and those around us – and some would add - a higher power. This is the "soulfulness" that Thomas Moore talked about – the feeling that we belong on this planet - that we have a purpose for being here; that we have a greater meaning in our lives that is embedded in our everyday activities that create within our normal lives a sense of fulfillment. I will talk about soulfulness and the growth of spirit much more completely in Chapter 9 when I discuss ways to become authentic.

The *third* way that you prepare for thriving is how you learn to deal with physical needs of your body as it attempts to heal and cope with disease. This process involves educating yourself about your disease and the treatment, and exploring many new sources of information, no matter how far beyond the usual. This includes ignoring dire predictions about your future while you give yourself what you need. And when you let others know that you are choosing to focus on living, it is not because you are denying the realities of your disease. It is because you are a living person, just as they are.

In transitioning into thriving you will gain control over the fear that you are surely doomed to an early death. You will line up your support in a way that promotes health and soulfulness, and, you will begin to get your healing routines set. You will not learn everything at once. You will never be the world's most perfect person, and no human being should ever strive for perfection. You will discover that the goal of becoming a thriver is a life-long process that is exciting.

As you read through the rest of this book, absorbing the information meant to help you in your route to thriving, begin to reflect continually on what you have in your life now, and what you have to look forward to if you are granted another day of healthy life. You are blessed to have an opportunity to find personal and spiritual meaning that is denied to others who have never faced your crisis, and to discover that the illusive meaning that you may have been looking for all your life is now right under your nose. Do you want to live? Then begin the journey now. What else do you have to do today that is more important?

THE
SECOND
CHALLENGE:

Learning That Help Lies Within You And All Around You

Since your birth, you have never been alone, even though at times you may have felt terribly adrift. Whether you know it or not, you have always have had with you two important sources of healing and comfort. The first is derived from the knowledge and expertise that has always been part of your personal, internal being, and that you will always find when you go inside to gain access to it. The second is the wisdom, healing power, and life-lessons that are yours, without charge, taken from the many spiritual practices available to you. In these five chapters I will teach you about these sources of help and healing in a way that you can begin to use them today. In their practice you will arise to a new state of health beyond what you have ever known before.

Chapter 5

Prayer

There is beginning scientific evidence that shows the value of prayer on mental and physical health. Despite that, the reason most people pray, is not because they trust in the scientific findings, but because their experience has taught them that prayer is a comforting practice in times of turmoil and crisis. Countless patients with whom I have worked have become convinced that prayer has supported and restored them during a health crisis, and has even resulted in maintaining health in the face of a dreadful prognosis. It was my patients who convinced me that prayer could have the most inconceivable consequences.

Ken

Twelve years ago, I visited Ken in the intensive care unit. His HIV had progressed into an infection that had invaded his blood, and was quickly shutting down all his organs. He was critically ill, and I felt that this was probably the last time I would see him alive. But instead, he told me that he was going to recover in time to join a candlelight vigil for people who had died of AIDS that would be held in four weeks on the grounds of the State Capitol. With a great deal of pride, he told me that two different churches were praying for him, and so were many of his friends. I said I thought that was great, but privately, I thought, "Okay, this is a long shot." Four weeks later, there was Ken at the vigil, weak and supported by friends to stand, but he was there.

Will

Will, who was on an inpatient unit where I was a consultant, had serious heart disease. He asked his family, doctors and nurses to pray for him. He wanted to live so that he could walk his daughter down the aisle at her wedding in two months time. Will was connected to every tube and monitor imaginable, and nobody could foresee such a recovery, but everyone got behind him and lent him their prayers. In the nurses' station, there was frequent conversation about Will's motivation to live, and it was so clear that all the staff were on his side, and had actually began to believe that he would have his prayers answered. He was discharged in time for his daughter's wedding. I lost track of him, so I do not know what happened after that, but the miracle that everyone had prayed for had already been granted.

Both meditation and prayer appear to improve mental and physical health by effecting changes in metabolic processes. Opinion polls show that most Americans believe in the healing power of prayer. I have worked with so many patients with cancer and HIV who have discovered prayer, and felt that their own prayers and other's prayers for them meant the difference between life and death. I could give many examples here. Fifteen years ago, as part of my community service work at the university, I held classes to help teach the facts of HIV disease to teams of interfaith volunteers from churches around the city. A large number of churches banded together to share their efforts in organizing people to give support to those in the late stages of AIDS. Many of these churches would hold prayer services for the patients under their care. Patients who requested prayers said they felt up-lifted and energetic for days afterward. Since that time, I have worked with a great many people who were not the recipients of organized efforts, but rather were at the center of many prayers offered by friends and family.

Carla

Knowing that I had survived my poor prognosis, I was the first person that Carla called when they determined that it was cancer that was behind her extreme fatigue and shortness of breath. Her grim diagnosis was metastatic, small cell lung cancer, the most fatal of all lung cancers. By the time it was discovered, it was already widely disseminated to her chest and her brain. Like so many patients with this form of cancer, she had a prognosis of less than 6 months to live, but Carla lived for 8 years before she died.

Shortly after diagnosis, Carla began, with her family and church a process of praying for recovery. Against all odds, Carla began to recover her health, and subsequent tests showed that the tumor in her brain and the tumors in her lungs were no longer visible on scans. During those 8 years she received palliative chemotherapy three times to help shrink the tumors. It is well-known that chemotherapy is not a cure for small-cell lung cancer, but it will sometimes extend life for an unspecified period of time, usually not a long period of time. Carla believed that her medical treatment helped her greatly, but while she could not prove it, she felt in her heart that prayer was at the top of the list as being the thing that made the most difference.

Many of us in health care fields have seen evidence of powerful forces for whose existence we have no scientific proof. Something not yet understood steps in for some people at times when they have almost abandoned hope. What is prayer, and what purpose does it serve in our lives? Prayer is a petition, entreaty, or a conversation with a power, usually a higher power. In prayer, we talk to a power, which by the way, does not have to be God. We can also direct prayers to the universe or simply to an unknown force. We can also talk to the power within ourselves, directing our prayers to our own inner wisdom. So many people say that they do not know how to pray, or what to say. Frankly I don't think it matters what you say. What is important is that you are engaging in a very loving act on behalf of yourself or another person, and casting out to the universe or to God your entreaties for a person's life and well-being. There are a myriad of explanations about why prayer works. Certainly most people who pray believe that we are in the care of a loving God or universe that listens to our heartfelt petitions. But a number of people have also advanced the plausible explanation that when we put forth positive thoughts, those thoughts become part of the world in which we live, and their intentions will now inhabit the very air we breathe. These two explanations may exist side-by-side. We can believe either without compromising belief in the other. Our own and other's thoughts and prayers profoundly affect our existence. Similarly, this is why negativity toward self and others needs to be rooted out of our thoughts.

So, positive or negative, our thoughts and prayers for ourselves and others become our wishes and our divine portion, which then becomes our reality. It is perfectly conceivable that negative thoughts toward others are the same as negative prayers, because when we think of another person in negative ways that is our prayer for that person's life. It is important, whether we are sick or well to be ever aware of the different ways that we can turn our thoughts and prayers in positive directions that are focused on the good. I believe that we do this by making a habit of it, by making regular time in our day to engage in positive thought or prayer, even if it is just for a small amount of time each day. In this way, a minute or two of being positive becomes a habit that spills over to the rest of the day.

Regularly engaging one's whole mind in some sort of prayer or positive supplication is a way of keeping well and as such it is well worth our time. Many years ago, I purchased a small chime that has a valued place on my dinner table. It reminds me before each meal to stop before a meal and send out positive thoughts for all who need them that day, including me. Along with whoever is joining me at the table, I think about members of my family, my friends, even the people I was less than loving to in the last 24 hours, and say a small prayer for their health and happiness. Believing as I do that thoughts and intentions are the most powerful thing we possess, the form of prayer that I like for the healing of other people goes like this:

> *I pray for the health and well-being of my sister or brother (say name). If it be good for her and others, I ask that prayers for a complete recovery be granted. I ask for her continued improvement, and for all blessings to surround her. I pray for a sense of peace, love, and power to envelop her and give her hope and strength. I also pray for myself, that I may live with continued happiness and abundant energy.*

If the prayer is for your own healing, I suggest that you think of what you want your prayer to accomplish. Try to make your intention as clear as possible. In thinking about what you want to include in your prayer, remember that you are a whole person with a whole life, and with a new challenge that you are still trying to understand and use for your growth. You are not just an ill person with an unfortunate internal disease that you want rid of as soon as possible, so you can go on and grind out your life as before. After you decide what you want your prayer to accomplish, write it out, and use it as a continual reminder to pray regularly. Add to it every once in awhile. As your understanding unfolds and your direction on life changes, similarly expand your ideas of what you want your prayers to accomplish.

Please do not be too caught up in searching out correct language, or overly worried about making a gross error in what you pray for. So much of the benefit of prayer will come from analyzing your intention, and clarifying your relationships with God or the universe and other humans in your life, not from the actual words you come up with. Your intention will come through for healing in all aspects of your existence. If you are unused to praying, and you are having trouble clarifying your intentions, I suggest that you just start by saying,

> *I don't know how to pray yet. I am not even sure what I need to ask for, but I know that I need a great deal of help to begin healing, and to begin to understand what I am going through. Help me. Amen.*

35

When you are in the early stages of your diagnosis, it might facilitate your goals if you ask family members and friends to pray for you. Not only will the prayers themselves be helpful, letting others help you will bond you together. So many people who know about your illness will ask you what they can do for you. Frequently, when neither of you can think of anything in particular, you both let it go, the offer never comes again, and the person, who could have been part of your life, drifts into a peripheral relationship with you. In saying a prayer, they are doing something concrete for you that will act as the glue that pulls you into a common purpose of healing, love, and caring. Moreover, it will enrich the person praying enormously, as the giver of the gift is always as blessed as the receiver.

Chapter 6

Meditation

Meditation is a personal experience in which one releases the continuous random and persistent thoughts that move though our heads continuously. Its aim is to move us to a higher state of consciousness, a finer vibration of energy. My friend and meditation teacher, Faith Babbitt, says that meditation is a way of learning to listen to your heart. From the time we wake up until the time we go to sleep, we are listening to our emotions and the constant chatter in our heads.

Most of us are so caught up in our activity-driven self-talk that we fail to recognize that human beings are born with the capacity to discover the wonderful wisdom that has accumulated from the ages, from our own history and from that of all human kind. We are absolutely driven by our false sense of time. We are so deluded in the notion that the past, present, and future are distinct from each other, that we fail to recognize that we have the past and the future living in us at each moment, and that we have the capacity to call on all human knowledge to guide our actions and to aid in healing.

Having cleared out the clutter from our persistent thoughts and emotions, we are in a position to hear and acknowledge whatever understanding comes forth to aid us in healing and protection. Meditation can teach us how to love more dearly ourselves and others. It can help us reach deeply within toward areas of knowledge and strength that we never knew existed. It can help calm us and give us renewed energy for growth. It can boost endorphin levels, creating better immune system functioning. You may wonder, as I have so many times, how sitting there doing nothing can result in so much good. And, to most of us raised in Western thinking patterns, meditation is exactly like nothing - no thinking, feeling, driving ourselves to achieve something - just doing nothing.

It is so hard to introduce meditation to people who have never done it and to whom it seems a total and complete waste of time. But I ask you to try it every day for a month. Even if you can only devote a few minutes to it on some days, you will begin to experience events in your life differently and note increased confidence and problem-solving ability. I was very reluctant to begin meditating. I found the livelier imaging, as covered in the next chapter, to be immediately useful, and took to it like a pig to mud. I have always been an active "fixer" of problems. Sitting back, passively and letting something happen, was very difficult for me. It took many tries to get involved in meditation so that I could finally experience its benefits. Meditation interrupts my worries for a little while, and allows me to shove my ever-present "to do" lists to the back burner. I have used meditation over the years to help me make crucial decisions. As a writer and a teacher, I am dependent upon words to get information across. Yet, I have found many times that words fail me when it comes to achieving a greater understanding of the issues that I am working with or worrying about. When writing or teaching, an illusive concept may come to me in such an ill-formed, vague state. When I sit down to meditate, I let go of trying to puzzle out the problem with words. I find in going back to it later that what before had been so nebulous would come easily. Through meditation, I attain tacit insight, an intuitive understanding that does not need to rely on language to gain admittance to one's grasp of truth.

It was through meditation that I finally began to get a clue as to how my own illness and my work with others who were ill were coming together to form an entirely new me. It was only after these insights came, that I finally could say with great honesty that I was grateful for my cancer diagnosis, and it was at that point too, that I was sure that having cancer would not drag me down. I discovered that I still had much to learn while on this earth. This may be hard for you to believe if you are newly diagnosed, but I gave up worrying about how much longer I would live. Comparing the me that was before and after, I figured that there is no way that I would want to go back to the way I was before, even to avoid all the fear and suffering that I went through. Now 25 years post diagnosis, I continue to study and learn better how to perform this seemingly simple act. I am not a meditation teacher. I am simply a learner, and as a fellow learner, I seek not to be your guru, but to be one of your supporters as you discover personal truths and new ways of healing.

Western culture does not prepare many of us for the quiet, passive experience of meditation. Another aspect of our culture that makes meditation difficult, for some of us, is that we feel falsely that we do not own our own time - it belongs to someone else. For so many of us, something that is not done for the people depending upon us, and results in no measurable achievements, will be the last thing we can justify. When you meditate, no one outside the self can see how it might make life better.

Before you leave the last paragraph, think about how all this applies to you. When is the last time you sat down and just gave to yourself a gift of time, time that you did not have to account for to anyone else? While you are thinking, I ask that you remember that your time is your life. If people can take all your time from you, perhaps they have stolen your life, too. I know, you do enjoy being of service to your family and others. You also will enjoy being of service to yourself and knowing that what you give to yourself benefits all those around you, as the evidence of the light of health and happiness within you begins to glow ever more strongly. To begin to take some of your life for yourself, announce to the entire family that you will not be available for a whole hour every day so that you can meditate, pray, or do imaging. Go to a place that you will begin to use for meditation, a place where you will feel relaxed and comfortable. Do not allow interruptions. Be very, very firm. Okay? This is your time and your life. A crucial step in healing is that you begin to acknowledge yourself as a person of inestimable value, and to learn that you are worthy of the time you are spending in self-discovery.

The three chapters covering prayer, meditation, and imaging are not long, and they are meant to be read as a group. For people with a life-threatening illness, they are usually combined. Within a given session, you can go from prayer, to imaging, then to meditation. Too, for all three, you will need to know about deep breathing and relaxation. Correct breathing and relaxation are the most important gifts we can give ourselves, whether used with prayer, imaging, meditation, or by themselves.

Meditation comes to us from many different traditions, Buddhism, Hinduism and Christianity, for a few. I remember how moved I was when meditating among Buddhists in Austin, Texas. I am not Buddhist, but every so often there would be open meditations in an outdoor rotunda. Several hundred of us would gather at sunrise to kneel and meditate. The soft roar of the Ohms, ranging from the deep men's voices to the higher women's chant was the most moving thing I have ever been part of. In my acupuncture classes at the College of Oriental Medicine, the professors would begin each class with a 20 minute meditation, a practice that relaxed us and set our minds toward learning.

Back at the university, I would watch my exhausted students come to my evening class from their days that had often begun in the clinical area 12 hours before the class started. In this secular, rarefied setting, I dared not begin the class with a meditation for fear that there would be a major complaint to the dean. One day, when in the middle of a lecture, noting the fatigue and boredom on the faces of my students, I stopped and asked them to all stand. I took them slowly through a series of Tai Chi warm-ups, and instructed them on how to breathe while they were doing them. When they sat back down, the increased energy level and interest in the material was palpable. Where they had sat in a wearied, slumped posture before, they now had their hands in the air, asking to participate. I, too felt renewed, and my teaching reflected abundant enthusiasm. After that, if I ever forgot to begin with the exercises, a student would remind me.

Although much of our knowledge about the practice of meditation comes from Eastern traditions, each of us can develop our own ways of meditating using varied self-suggestions and physical postures. In reviewing the literature on this subject, I have found it to be rife with authoritative "thou shall nots." But I do not believe, for example, that your back absolutely must be as straight as an arrow, nor that your hands must be turned up, with the thumb and first finger in an O configuration, nor that you have to be in a yoga posture. Some of these positions will put you in a receptive pose, but the only vital thing about posture is that you should let yourself relax into a sitting or lying down position that is as comfortable as possible.

HOW TO START MEDITATING

If your health permits, stand up and stretch while doing deep breathing. Even when bed-ridden, people can stretch limbs to some extent, especially the shoulders and back. Reposition yourself for comfort throughout the meditation if your body is calling to you.

Correct breathing is one of the most important things we can do for our health. For centuries, the breath has been part of the meditation experiences of many Eastern meditative traditions, including Chinese Medicine, Buddhism, and Yoga. The breath is one of the most effective ways of renewing healing energy, but it would only give you energy to engage in whatever activities you have planned for that day, it would be worth the few seconds it takes to breathe correctly. It needs to be part of every meditation and relaxation exercise.

When starting to meditate it is important that the breath come from the stomach up to the top of the chest, not in short gasps from the chest. The lower abdomen should expand greatly with each intake of breath, and diminish and empty as you exhale. Yoga practitioners believe that when

40

we breathe correctly, healing energy, or "prana," enters the body with every inhalation, then used up energy departs with every exhalation. From a Western perspective, deep breathing results in a balance of oxygen and carbon dioxide. It is important to note your breathing, especially when you are expecting the results of medical tests, or taking in any news, positive or negative, about your health. Waiting to exhale decreases needed oxygen. Shallow and frequent breaths take their toll because they decrease the amount of carbon dioxide in our bodies, and we end up in the highly anxious state called, "hyperventilation." If you can only do one thing for your health today, please breathe correctly.

Meditation always begins with relaxation and focusing on the breath, a focus that is maintained throughout the meditation session. Put your hands together on your abdomen, and as your abdomen expands in inhalation, your hands should separate and feel like a balloon that is filling up with air. After the abdomen expands, then let the air travel up to fill the top of your lungs. If there is no nasal obstruction that prevents this, breathe in through your nose and out through your mouth, with lips slightly pursed to create a very small breath sound that is faintly audible. Some experts suggest that you arch your back slightly as you inhale, and flatten it upon exhaling. At first, do this ever so slightly, as it is a form of exercise that can create muscle soreness if you are not used to it. The most important thing is to be relaxed about breathing.

After assuming the position you will use to meditate, take two to three long, deep stomach breaths and hold each of them for a few seconds, before you exhale. When you are fully relaxed, check your body for tension and prepare yourself to listen. If a stray thought or worry comes in, just brush it away in your mind, or quickly acknowledge it, by saying to yourself, "thought," and let it go. The idea is to arrive at the state of "focus on nothing," that will be the most effective condition for meditation. Throughout the meditation, don't be concerned if nothing seems to be happening. Something is happening to your body and your mind.

If you wish, you may start your meditation by posing a question that you would like answered during the meditation. After posing it, forget about it. The answer may come to you during the meditation, but it probably will not. Later you will find that you have the knowledge you were seeking, when something that has been puzzling you for a long time becomes as clear as glass. A meditation can last from 10 minutes to an hour, so set the time you want to spend in meditation beforehand, and you will return to full consciousness after you have been meditating for that length of time.

I hope you will set a schedule of regular meditation, starting today, and that you will seek out experiences in your community that will teach you more and more about this ancient and effective practice. People who have a life-threatening diagnosis are in turmoil and in change. Many of us are acutely aware that our diagnosis portends a possible loss of our life, and that we may die before we are ready to go. In our apprehension and anxiety, we may temporarily lose the grasp of who we are, and in fact, often find ourselves worrying about what will become of us. At times we wish we could go back to being just who we were before, but that is not an option, as we find ourselves on the other side of a barrier that our friends and families have never crossed. The chasm we have traversed is so wide, that we feel our messages get lost in having to shout across a gap of miles to those on the other side. Having been separated in some important ways from our loved ones by the fear and the new insight our illness is delivering, we struggle for ways to merge our two lives without losing ourselves or our valued relationships in the process.

Happily because of where it leads us, our crisis so often turns out to be the opportunity to be more than we ever were. But it is painful to lose the self, even for a little while. Something needs to step in and support us through this time of turmoil and uncertainty. Meditation is one of the most powerful tools you have to help you through this. As you will see, positive outcomes for mental, physical, and spiritual health are found in the breath, in total relaxation, and in openness to experience. Too, from a very practical standpoint, the process of carving out the time for meditation is part of constructing a structure that allows you to value yourself and give time to yourself, time that before you may before have considered a selfish, therefore a wasteful expenditure of your energy and efforts.

I hope I have convinced you that meditation is something, not nothing. In contrast, science and progress have provided us with innumerable gadgets, toys and food that are nothing. So if you want something, try meditating. If you want nothing, go to your favorite coffee house and pay five dollars for a decaf, non-fat latte with artificial sweetener.

Chapter 7

Imaging Your Health

It matters not how straight the gate,
How charged with punishments the scroll,
I am the master of my fate:
I am the captain of my soul.
-William Ernest Henly

Imaging or visualization is seeing with the mind something that is not in direct sight, even something inside our bodies. I have an image of my own heart, yet I have never seen it. Each of us has mental images of parts of ourselves and our total selves. Most of these are pretty well fixed, but others are continually changing with the input of environmental circumstances. Our images of ourselves and the world have a powerful effect on our behavior - on who we think we are and how we then behave. What we have in our minds over a period of time eventually becomes our reality. Through believing in ourselves, we can in truth become the captain of our souls.

Bob

It turns out that illness is a potent force for the changing of self-image - usually not for the better at first. Bob was only 44 at the time of his first heart attack. He was an advertising executive, who was at the top of his field. He got to the top because of his talent, but also he knew how to sell himself and his work in a confident way. Even after being on the road to recovery, he still saw himself as weak and one-down. His voice became reedy and sad. His posture was stooped and accompanied by lifeless gestures. He was considering changing fields or going for early retirement. I asked him to close his eyes and tell me what he saw as his image of himself, and then how he was imaging his disease within his body. He said,

> My image of myself is as a very tiny person. Everyone else is large in comparison. When I speak, nobody can hear me. I see myself as an old man, useless and spent. The problems with my circulation make my arteries feel like my adversary. My heart is damaged and failing me. I see the rest of me under the control of this horrible malfunctioning thing. On the other hand I love my heart. It is the only heart I have. I want to care for it, cure it.

Bob had transformed having heart disease into being heart disease. He saw his heart as weak and vulnerable; he saw himself the same way. Yet, we see the glimmer of potential for healing in the last part of his answer when he says, "I love my heart." When first diagnosed, most of us hate or mistrust the offending organ or disease process that has threatened our lives. With a great deal of help, we finally realize that our disease is part of us, too, and is the part that we most need to accept and image into health. The following precepts lie behind the success of imaging in disease:

- Already existing within your body are the seeds for healing yourself.
- The force for health that is contained in you is more powerful than your disease.
- You possess all the knowledge that you need to heal yourself.
- You deserve to have perfect health – it is your right.

We are imaging all the time. You may wonder why we should have to learn imaging if is something that we are already doing. So it is important to understand that the images that occur from blows to your body or to your self-esteem are out of your control, and do not always serve your best interest in either healing or getting along in life. Conversely, deliberate imaging allows you to guide these powerful self-portrayals so that those that affect directly the prognosis of your illness and your whole approach to life can be guided by developing optimism and hope instead of despair and fear. For example, if while undergoing treatment for your illness, you think, "I have cancer, and nothing can stop it. I am dead" you are interfering with the constructive outcome that your rational mind is seeking.

Professional and amateur athletes and trainers have long discovered the benefits of imaging for improving athletic skills and accuracy. People in professional sports are ever focused on results. Accordingly, they would not stick with a method that did not work. My first experience with the physical power that comes from imaging occurred when I took a class on Qi Gong, which is a system of energy healing that comes to us from China. Four small women, each using only their outstretched fingers on both hands, lifted a man who must have weighed more than 200 lbs, by imaging him as light. I could hardly believe it, so I volunteered to be in the next group of "lifters." I was astonished at how easy it was. He felt like a feather. Everyone who tried it was giddy from the enormity and the unreality of the experience. I was impressed then, and continue to be impressed about the power that imaging has to make a feat lighter, to make a task easier, and to make an impact on every single thing we attempt to do. Michael Crichton, author of *Jurassic Park*, and many other books, participated in several sessions in which he described how he learned to bend spoons, using the images in his mind. When lifting something heavy or bending spoons, we can see with our own eyes that imaging does produce very tangible results. Seeing a demonstration of imaging like the lifting of the 200 lb man was important to help me understand that imaging actually works. Now, even when I cannot see what I am imaging with my own eyes, I still have confidence that the results I visualize in my mind are actually taking place. When you have a personal experience with the effects of imaging on your body you will experience a dramatic increase in healing and physical and emotional energy.

Negative images are always with us after a serious diagnosis. It is important to turn these appalling prophesies around to something more affirming as soon as you can. Fortunately, imaging helps us do this, and happily too, the process of imaging is not difficult. The small amount of time that it takes makes it possible for anyone to do it, anytime, anywhere. If I ask you now to image your favorite dessert, you could do so in a flash. Thinking of it now, I can see the double-double chocolate cake, dripping with soft white chocolate icing, with a creamy scoop of vanilla ice cream on top. When I wrote this, my mouth started watering in response. This is a physiological reaction to a picture in the mind. Stop and try this yourself. If I can create a physical response in my salivary glands so quickly just from thinking about chocolate cake, can I not do this anywhere in my body by learning how?

You can engage in active imaging anytime – before a meeting, while driving your car, when waiting for appointments, before dropping off to sleep, or I have to say it, while sitting on the john or standing in the shower. Influencing our thoughts in these ways presets every experience to be positive. Early in my treatment, I would sit in my doctor's waiting room, dreading my chemotherapy. The visit would start with the nurse drawing my blood. Then I sat and waited, holding my breath, for the results, to see how badly the last chemo had depleted me and if I could go on with my treatment that day. Finally, while the doctor was injecting the drugs into a vein in my hand, I would anticipate the awful taste I would have in my mouth when the drugs entered my bloodstream. This was followed by images of the fatigue, nausea, and dragging down of my mind that would follow each treatment for a few days. Such was the idea of my treatment that I was taking into every session with my doctor. Imaging this experience now, after 20 years, I can still feel pain and taste the toxicity of the drugs. Back then, I knew that I had to do something to turn this around. I could not go on with a full year of treatment with this negative view of what was supposed to help me. My attitude was not only creating much suffering, but also I became convinced that it was interfering with my treatment outcome.

Finally, at my oncologist's suggestion, I picked up a copy of Simonton's book. As long ago as 1978, a radiation oncologist named O. Carl Simonton learned through experiences in his own practice that cancer and other diseases were diseases of the whole person. In his book, *Getting Well Again*, he laid out an approach to cancer treatment based upon imaging the demise of your disease by conjuring up aggressive images like *pac man*. His primary thesis was that how you participate, mentally, in your own healing makes the critical difference between living and dying. He presented many case studies of patients whose cancer underwent a remission that was totally unexplained and unexpected. Even then, I saw Simonton's method as going beyond how you image healing your disease. I could apply his principles to any situation in which I anticipated a negative outcome, including how I approached every situation in which I had to confront life as a cancer patient. Since 1978, Simonton's methods have moved into the mainstream of treatment. This has been aided so much by the efforts of surgeon, Dr. Bernie Siegel, who been very effective in bringing Simonton's work into medical practice.

I know that imaging works. For one thing, I do not propose something in this book that I have not personally used myself with success. I have felt the healing effects of imaging in my own life and have born witness to its miracle of healing in so many others. I have no hesitation in telling you that this is absolutely and unequivocally among the most effective of all the treatment modalities for physical and emotional disease that I have discovered. I used relaxation tapes that I made myself, with guided images that had specific and important meanings to me to rejuvenate my energy and increase my hope when I was undergoing simultaneous chemotherapy and radiation, and for many years after that. I begin to image my treatment as life-saving, and I turned around the negative approach I was taking to it. As the drugs entered my body, I visualized them as my saviors, attacking cancer cells and destroying them

There is a great deal of evidence concerning how positive and negative messages become self-fulfilling prophecies. Imaging is a very flexible technique that can be done with relaxation, meditation or prayer or along with each of them. I prefer to use imaging with guided meditation and relaxation. This is also called "guided imagery." Most of the imaging/visualization tapes that exist are based on this form of visualization. It is very possible, perhaps even preferable, to learn to visualize without benefit of a professional tape. You may decide to use one of these at first, but I think as soon as you are comfortable, it is important to guide yourself through all these steps, and I will show you how. If you decide to use a professionally made tape, you can find them in any large bookstore. Some of the tapes I have found most helpful are by Emmett E. Miller, Louise L. Hay, and Bernie Siegel, although this is not an exhaustive list of the good ones.

There are many ways to image/visualize that affect disease. You can try different approaches until something feels like it is yours. For me, in order to get the absolute most benefit from imaging, I use it as part of a set of healing methods that I will cover in the rest of this chapter. These include: correct breathing techniques; use of the white light of healing; relaxation and progressive relaxation; accessing a spirit guide or your inner intelligence; directing energy; and giving yourself auto-suggestions before ending the session. I offer this approach to you now as a way of starting you off on your new and exciting adventure that will occur completely inside your own mind and body.

Breathing. In Chapter 6 we learned that centered breathing is the beginning, the middle, and the end of all relaxation, meditation, and imaging. If you do it as a start to every meditation or visualization session, you will learn that your relaxation begins with the first breath. It becomes the stimulus from which follows the relaxation response.

White Light of love, healing and protection. Visualize yourself as sitting or lying in a cocoon of white light, and then see the light as moving around you and through you. It does not matter whether you actually believe that you are creating a light, or whether you think you are imagining it. Either way, it works as a healing presence and a source of energy that is both healing and protective. This image is soothing. It shields you from negative energy from within and from without. It allows you to shed the influences that the rest of the world have on you for a little while, to close the door to interferences on your healing time with yourself.

Holding the image of yourself in the light also allows you to put away the painful emotions that have their hold on you. As you invite the white light to surround you, put aside your pain and let go of your hurt while you open yourself up to higher energies and magnificent possibilities. When you call on the white light for protection, you have started a process of healing that moves you far beyond a focus on your disease. Stop reading this now, and just for a few minutes, visualize yourself surrounded by white light. See yourself in a cone of white light, safe and secure from all harm and all negativity. Let yourself relax and enjoy the quiet feeling that comes from this experience.

Anytime you find yourself with any degree of tension, whether you are trying to get to sleep or when driving your car in heavy traffic, surround yourself with a cone of white light and attune to correct breathing. Anytime you experience fear, you can call on the white light of healing and protection, and let yourself bask in its healing power.

Relaxation. Both meditation and visualization depend upon relaxation. In the early 1970s, I was introduced to a book that opened my mind to the rich possibilities of relaxation, Barbara Brown's *New Mind, New Body*. Dr. Brown, a physiological psychologist and an early advocate and practitioner of biofeedback expounded the thesis that deep relaxation could be measured as alpha brain waves. It turned out that through deep relaxation, in an alpha state, people could control such autonomic nervous system functions as lowering their pulse and blood pressure, and raising the temperature in their hands. All these physiological changes affect the internal workings of our body.

Relaxation is beneficial in itself. It decreases anxiety, decreases tension and fatigue, increases mental clarity, opens you to a state of receptiveness for healing, and acts as a helper for any other healing method you are using. I have practiced and taught a modified form of Brown's autogenic training for many years as a way of becoming completely relaxed. Autogenic training focuses on three states: *quiet, heavy*, and *warm*. I will use these three key words when I help you build your own meditation. Suffice to say here, to get the most from guided imagery, you need to be in as relaxed a state as circumstances permit. Interestingly, you cannot will yourself into being relaxed. Relaxation comes when you passively "let it come." So in the meditation that follows when I say, "Let your arms relax," that is just what I mean – just think about it while you let it happen.

Calling for Help from Within: Your Center of Wisdom. Several years ago, when I lived in San Antonio, Texas, out of curiosity, I took several courses from a psychic who taught at the Women's Resource Center, Faith Babbitt. Her course covered awareness patterns, such as meditation, auras, intuition, and meeting your spirit guide. Even though I came from a long tradition of energy healing and imaging, I must admit that I was very skeptical about psychic phenomena, and to a moderate extent, I still am. Faith was an excellent teacher, and extraordinarily gifted. She was also possessed of a simple conviction about the good of all people on the earth, and was full of love for the earth and all on it. There was neither an exploitive nor an entrepreneurial bone in her body. Although she was filled with a good common sense advice that arose from her philosophy of universal love, caring, harmony, forgiveness, and truth, non-the-less she did not convince me that she could help me to see into my future with any great consistency. What she taught me well was how to go inside myself for help in a way that has boosted my confidence and my ability to trust myself in my own meditations. One of the most important lessons that she taught was how I could go inside and find help from what she and many writers have called my "spirit guide."

What Faith called spirit guides, you can also think of as your "center of wisdom." I did a meditation session with Faith in which I met my guide and was able to receive verbal answers to the questions that I posed. You may think of this voice as a guide or angel; as something or someone who has come from the spirit world to help you; as a facet of your current religion; or simply as your own wisdom that you are allowing to come through while you are in a relaxed self-hypnotic state. What is important in sessions of guided imagery is that you will be able to pose your questions, and access the keys to your healing from the vast wisdom that is contained within you and is there for your use anytime.

In guided imaging the idea of the spirit guide is useful in helping you to decide many things about your health and your treatment, and it can help you very much as you work to influence the outcome of your disease. After you have achieved a relaxed state, I suggest that you go in your mind to a comfortable place, one that nourishes your mind and spirit, such as a river or a forest, and when you get there in your mind, call for someone to appear who can help you with your questions or can give sound advice. At times when I do this, I hear the answer right away, and at other times, it comes later, though usually within the same day. According to Faith Babbitt, we are never alone in our turmoil. We can always go within and ask for help and receive it.

The Meditation

Now I will put together for you all the above elements to form a suggested meditative exercise that will allow you to begin your guided image session. This is only one of the many forms of guided imagery that are available in books and on tapes. Please do not try to read this while doing visualization. Read it over several times and try to do your session on your own or ask a friend to read the suggestions. You can also use this example to make a recording for your session. It is nice to select your favorite quiet music and play that as background during your session.

BREATHE: Sit in a relaxed position. As you sit or lie there, let your mind clear of all the daily distractions, and begin your *breathing*. Take a deep stomach breath through your nose, holding it for a bit and letting it out through your mouth slowly. Take a second breath, holding it a little longer before expelling. Finally take a third breath and hold it as long as you can before expelling it with a rapid force, completely emptying your lungs.

WHITE LIGHT: Call on the *white light* of protection to surround you, making you and your entire environment safe, calm, and secure. Lie in your pool of white light for a few minutes, experiencing the comfort that this brings.

RELAX: Begin your relaxation by saying to yourself: *"I am feeling quite quiet. I am beginning to feel quite relaxed."* Let your whole body go into a restful relaxed mode. Then you will begin, in turn, to relax different parts of your body, limbs, and face. Start with your right arm. Let your right arm become *quiet*. Then feel it as very *heavy*, so heavy that you could hardly lift it if you wanted to. Then, beginning with the fingers of that hand, gradually let your right arm become very *warm*. When you have completed that arm to your satisfaction, move to the other arm, then in turn to each leg. Then start at the top of your head, and relax all the muscles in your head, your forehead, and your face. Feel your forehead becoming as smooth as glass. Relax the muscles in your jaws. Then starting at the top of your neck, go down your body, relaxing all the muscles in your neck, chest, back, stomach, and buttocks. Your eyelids are so heavy. You don't want to even try to open them because the forces keeping them closed are so much stronger than the forces that can open them.

IMAGE: See before you a door. Know that beyond the door is a space in which you will be entirely joyful, comfortable, safe, and relaxed. Slowly walk toward the door and go in. On this side you will see a place that is more beautiful and serene than any you have experienced before, populated with your favorite flowers, trees, animals, and perhaps a peaceful river, lake or stream. Find a place where you can be at ease, even if you have to bring in your own favorite chair, and sit down in comfort. You are here to heal your mind, body, and spirit. You are surrounded by the white light and sheltered in a lovely place. In the setting that you have created, there is all that you need for healing. Now visualize the disease or unwanted pattern that you want to heal. See it as clearly as you can.

Visualize what would help you to eliminate that pattern or disease. Use such things as the cells in your own immune system, or invent fish or animals that devour it, or something else, or just see the pattern or disease as containing what it needs for its own self-destruction. Watch it now as it is being eliminated, and say goodbye to it. Take as long as you wish for this process. You will do this again and again over the next few months. Some people have reported that they could not image the destruction of their disease. That is fine. Try some other things, like asking it not to harm you. Too, with time, you will learn your own ways to control disease and other unwanted patterns besides the ones I am suggesting here.

Visualize your body, bit by bit, starting with your head and moving down to your feet. Feel or sense any unwanted patterns, including disease, infection, pain, stress, fear, or anguish and feel them being smoothed over by the white light that surrounds you. See yourself as glowing in this light and restored to health in every way that is possible to be healthy. Remember, it is your right to have health.

GOING WITHIN FOR HELP AND ADVICE: When you have completed the guided healing exercise you are ready to call upon a guide or center of wisdom to be with you and answer any questions that you may have about any aspect of your life, including your health. If you do not want to use a guide, go deep within and call forth your highest sense of understanding and the latent knowledge that is there, but often inaccessible. Ask any question to which you need an answer. If you want to use a guide, ask your guide to appear. Picture this person as clearly as you can. Accept your guide in whatever form in which he or she appears. Ask, "What should I call you?" After hearing the name, pose any questions you have and wait for the answer. Know that you may not hear this aloud, but in your thoughts, or it will come to you after the healing session. Spend as long as necessary with your guide and before leaving, thank your guide for being with you.

When you are ready, give yourself a post-hypnotic suggestion that you will emerge from this session with abundant energy and an improved outlook on life. Slowly, in your mind, begin to count backward from 10, and wake up when you have reached one. Gently stretch, come back to full consciousness, and be ready for whatever you will confront.

Do your visualization exercises as often as possible. You do not have to do every aspect of what is above in every session. Anytime, even in the middle of a rush hour traffic jam, you can breathe, relax your muscles, and call forth the white light of love, protection, and healing. In some sessions, you may wish to just sit in the sacred place that you have created in your mind and meditate. Use prayer, meditation and guided imagery often to support your healing, calm your fears, and support the growth that you are seeking in yourself as a human being.

Chapter 8

Using Energy

Energy practices primarily derive from Eastern healing traditions. They are based on the view that you, along with every other living thing, are a complex field of life energy, involved in a constant interaction with surrounding energy fields. From this perspective health is defined as a balance in energy. So by deduction, disease is a state of imbalance in energy, resulting in a blockage, deficiency, or disequilibrium in the energy field. Imbalances can be felt, diagnosed, and treated by competent practitioners of acupuncture, shiatsu, healing touch, and other fields. It is not necessary to buy into the theory of energy fields in order to obtain help. No system of energy healing is based upon faith healing.

Holistic healing rests on the view that all humans have value. We create meaning in our lives through participation - our willingness to be in true service to others. Conversely, bitterness and anger that builds up inside can literately eat away at your health, undermining your own good thoughts and feelings day after day, until finally you become a mass of fuming thoughts. This does not mean that you have to tolerate the presence of people in your life who are not good for your physical, mental, and spiritual being. Instead you can send them positive energy in your mind and say to yourself, "I forgive you, I forgive myself, and I send you into the light." Thus we let go of both their presence in our lives and the antipathy that is forever retarding our attempts at healing.

I found energy healing, consisting of acupuncture and healing touch, to be valuable tools for lifting my spirits and moving me toward health. Acupuncture turned around my attitude toward cancer and toward the life that I would now live. As a "head in the sand scientist," I had always regarded these as "strange practices." But with experience, I learned that acupuncture works to heal the whole person, not just the disease. Oh, yes, you will find practitioners of this art who focus only on symptoms – toothaches, neck pain, and back pain - but they are not practicing the holistic science in which they were trained. Each acupuncture meridian has an emotional, a spiritual and a physical connection

If you cannot locate or afford a professional in this field, do not loose heart. There are many other approaches to energy work. When I was at my lowest, after having received almost 5000 rads of radiation to my chest, and about 1/4 of my chemotherapy, I attended a meeting of a group of women, many of whom were healers. Seeing my depleted state, one of the women asked the others to form a circle around me. They went into a dance and chant in which energy was directed toward lifting up my spirit and my physical energy. I have never in my life felt so much better in such a short time. The energy from that experience stayed with me for days after. I was convinced from that experience to do more energy work to keep up my vigor and vitality.

Many holistic methods are easy to learn. Yet, they universally are profoundly healing and comforting. I was called to the bedside of a woman in her 80s who was at the home of her daughter, and in the last stages of dying from cancer. Knowing that she was a highly religious Baptist, I hesitated about offering her therapeutic touch, a secular energy modality, but she said, "Go ahead, dear." I was in the middle of giving her a treatment when her doctor came by to see her. As always she was delighted to see her doctor, but she told him, "Don't come in now. This nurse is working on me." She went into a profound state of relaxation and found a freedom from pain and suffering that had up to then eluded her. Before leaving, I taught her daughter how to clear the energy field to decrease pain, and the daughter used that approach up until the moment of death to comfort her mother. Instead of feeling useless and helplessness when her mother's pain was out of control, she knew that there was something that she could always do to ease the suffering. This was literally a life-saver in caring for her mother.

Therapeutic Touch

Therapeutic touch is a healing technique in which you use your hands to heal. It presumes that each person is a complex field of energy. This field can be disturbed in a number of ways. It can be weak or distorted. It can be unbalanced from one side of the body to the other - that is, full or perhaps cold on one side, and empty or hot on the other. There have been many research studies done on this method in the field of nursing. When you follow the steps below and have a clear intention to heal, you will find that you are a healer. As a person with a serious disease, you may want to find a therapeutic touch practitioner to work with you, or have a family member learn the technique, following these steps:

Intentionality. Intentionality is the mind set that we bring into treatment to heal and produce a positive outcome in the treatment. It starts with clarifying in your mind your purpose for being there.

Centering. Centering means that you pull your mind and thoughts into full presence. When I center myself, I go through a brief relaxation exercise that I described in the last chapter. I start by saying "I feel quite quiet. I am beginning to feel quite relaxed." Then I clear my mind, relax any tension in my body, focus my thoughts in the present, and let go of any worries that I may have about anything.

Assessment. In assessment, you use your hands to go over the entire head and body of the person to whom you are giving the treatment. In therapeutic touch, you are not touching the skin of the person, but rather the energy field. Your hands are kept 2 – 3 inches away. You are looking for imbalance from one side of the body to the other, or in a specific location, in temperature or the force of the energy field. You may feel a pocket of heat or cold, tingling, pulsating, or pressure along the body or head. Different healers perceive energy differently. I feel energy depletion as tingling, while another healer may feel it as cold. Some patterns appear to be more or less universal among people I have treated. For example, when I experience a cold sensation in my fingers at the base of a person's skull, the person is almost always experiencing a moderate to severe depression.

Stand before the person, if they are sitting, and start at the top of the head, about 2-3 inches from the skin, and slowly go down toward the feet, feeling every bit of the person's energy field for signs of imbalance. After you assess the front of the body and head, go to the back, and then to each side. You can note each area of imbalance, and return to the area after the total assessment. It is important to follow this routine until you become highly skilled at the art of doing this. As an advanced practitioner, I now make the assessment and the treatment phase one seamless step, treating as I go along.

Directing Energy, Clearing the Field, and Ending the Treatment. Here you direct or transfer energy into the areas of the body that you have identified as needing treatment. You channel energy with your hands over the energy field, imaging energy from your hands to the affected part.

When I do this I always feel a glow in my hands as the energy is transferred. As you go through the process of treatment, you should not only be directing energy into the body, you should be clearing out areas where too much energy has collected. This clearing is called "sweeping" in some Hispanic cultures. It is also called "brushing." When you sweep or brush you use your hands in a sweeping manner to brush off excess energy. Many Therapeutic Touch practitioners will never channel energy into a very sick, debilitated, or dying person because too much reception of energy can be overwhelming to them – *they only use sweeping*. In those cases, you skip the assessment and treatment phases, and starting at the top of the head, slowly sweep down and away from the body several times. Any observer can see the relaxation response as people uncoil their legs and arms and stretch out in a relaxed pose. It is especially helpful for restlessness and pain. I will also teach the family to brush the energy field before an ill person eats to settle the stomach, a process that puts the patient in a receptive state to ingest food.

Chapter 9

Spirituality In Health And Illness

Almost of the material for this chapter is taken from my research studies and clinical practice with men and women who have HIV disease. I studied people who were in all stages of HIV disease, from newly diagnosed to those who were actively dying. Both the words and the sentiments of the men and women who were part of these studies are in what follows. I am so grateful for their part in advancing my increasing awareness of how the spirit unfolds in illness. I went into interviews with the attitude that they were my teachers. What was added to my own view of the human spirit was a thick and deep description from a vocal group who spoke from the heart and had a longing to teach, to pass on to the next generation their insights.

From Robert, a person with AIDS, 1995:

Denying validity to the learned doctor's opinions was my best choice given the prevailing circumstances. And these were going from bad to worse in the first part of the 1980s. The "Emperor Science" went clueless and cloakless to this affair. Deep-seated survival instincts now guided my ship, and escape from this madness was my destination.

Robert's was trying to find a way to survive the worst news that he had ever received in his life. After a brief period of what he called "denial," he began seeking a way out of the insanity of his plight. Having been an injecting drug user, he became clean and enrolled in graduate school. Ten years later the depth in his discovery of spirituality had been phenomenal. He made this statement about his life then:

> My faith came about through grace and the engagement of the process of change that was set before me. My own journey seemed long, and sometimes I think about past events and wonder how it is that I've come to be someone new.

Many of us leave our spirituality, what our lives mean, to philosophers and religious leaders. Yet, your spirituality, unlike your religion, cannot be handed down from a higher authority, because it involves a personal quest for meaning that lasts over a lifetime. In Robert's case, the less traveled path to his spiritual transformation was laid before him as a choice when he was jolted by the realization that he would not live forever – information that had never exactly been a secret, but it was not, before his diagnosis, ingrained into his personal philosophy. A serious diagnosis provoked the spiritual questions for Robert, and for all of us who share his health-related circumstances: Why is this happening to me? What am I supposed to do now? These questions finally directed him and will direct you to more questions: Who am I? Why am I on earth? What will happen to me? Why do I want to live?

You will never find the ultimate truth about your own life, and if anyone tells you that they have done so, they are missing something in all this. What you will find during your search for self and meaning is that there is neither a set of ultimate truths nor an end of the path that will culminate in finally knowing everything there is to know, and resulting in needing to learn no more. A vital purpose in life is to seek, to explore, to climb the mountain to see if you can. And the meaning that you find when you seek and explore is embedded in your activities of living – your relationships with self, others, and the universe or God.

In this chapter, I will suggest ways to search that will provide immense satisfaction in themselves, and that will uncover deeper and ever deeper meanings in your understanding of the purpose and the meaning of your life. Each answer you receive provokes more questions aimed at gradually unraveling the mysteries of living your ordinary life. The meaning of all of our lives rests in the ways that we live them day to day, week after week. There is not a lot about true spirituality that is transcendent and holy. And what you will see too is that it is the process of seeking that results in profound happiness and exhilaration. In this chapter, I will present a number of quotes from my interviews, because listening to their discoveries may provoke in you a similar theme that will spur you look at yourself differently.

Before your illness, you may never have awakened each day with the thought, "This day is precious. I will use it wisely." Before, time was something to pass or to squander unthinkingly. Eric Fromm said that in our culture, which is perhaps the first secularized culture in human history, we can start with the assumption that there is no purpose to life except to "get it over with without major mishaps." What our individual lives mean and what our obligations are to self and others are matters left to be solved by each person, ill or well without a lot of help or encouragement from health professionals or religious leaders. But there are some exceptions.

Dr. Wright and Clara

When I was doing my HIV research, I kept hearing from the participants about Dr. Wright, an HIV specialist, who was a very special physician indeed. He was caring in every way possible. One of my interview participants, Clara, was a 28 year old woman who had been leading a fast paced life of drugs, alcohol, and casual sex. At the same time she was the life of a party, she was a loner, holding herself back from any close relationships at all. Confused and on her own, she tried to deal with the fall out from her HIV diagnosis without any help whatsoever except for what Dr. Wright provided. She did not tell anyone for months that she was HIV positive, including her roommate. Dr. Wright helped her through the worst of her confusion and grief by listening to her, teaching her about her illness and its treatment, and letting her know that he cared about her as a human being of worth.

When Clara told Dr. Wright that she had not been close to her family in a long time, he still urged her to talk to them. He told her that he would help her tell them. Then Clara called her parents and asked them to come to Dr. Wright's office to talk about her health. He demystified HIV by casting it as a disease, just like any other disease that needed treatment, and he went though her treatment plan with them. He showed them how they could be supportive of her efforts at health. They all cried during that meeting. Even Dr. Wright had tears in his eyes. Afterward, Clara's folks asked her to move back home so that her life could be easier and so they could get to know her again. Her mother told me that she was grateful to have a chance to be a mother again.

Many good things happened to Clara after that. She joined a support group of women that Dr. Wright recommended. She now had a place where she could feel safe to laugh and cry. She basked in the love of her family. She found a better job that she liked and was competent at. She began to make a few nice friends from work and her group. From her new found position at the center of love, Clara moved from marching though life in a meaningless way, to a state of spirituality, learning to participate fully in each moment. She told me that she was the happiest she had ever been, and felt that she had finally become an adult. She said to me, "Sometimes now, I think I have a glow about me that anyone should be able to see. It feels so good to be this happy."

Many people confront the need for spiritual meaning for the first time when they are told they have serious illness. The transformations forced by illness give us a chance to realize why we were put here on earth, and give us an opportunity to find ways to love ourselves. Most of the people I have known who have a serious illness have told me that their illness was a gift. As Scott put it, "It was a gift. At first it was a gift I wanted to return, but it was a gift." HIV, in this man's life, caused him to foreground his unexamined fear of living. The gift was the revelation that he was put on earth to help other people. Never having spoken publicly before, he became an accomplished speaker, leading services at his church, speaking at school assemblies, to help kids prevent HIV. All his life, a mousey person who went unnoticed, he had found himself and his voice through his experience with illness.

Monica

Monica, who was newly diagnosed with cancer told me "My cancer was not, "just some fluke that got me; a punishment for some sin. It was something I was meant to have." For Monica it was a chance to reunite with a family made distant by anger and misunderstanding. It was an opportunity to move beyond a rather meaningless job in which she had been just going to work to pay the bills, and coming home to get rest so that she could go to work to pay the bills. She went back to school part time to become a computer analyst, started her own business at home, and found that she had plenty of time and energy to volunteer at her church and a local hospice. Her new life, filled for the first time with meaning and time to live, convinced her that she was better off having cancer than not having cancer.

Daniel

Daniel was one of my research participants. He ran a support group for persons with HIV. He said,

> Religion is a lot about how I express my spirituality.
> It gives me a belief structure from which to work. But now
> I have developed my personal rituals – I sit and drink tea
> every morning while I watch the birds. I facilitate a support

group. I work with children. Those are expressions of my spirituality, which have become more and more about understanding my commitments not only to God but to myself and to other people.

My research and practice with ill people have convinced me that the link between religion and spirituality is that religion can provide the words to express spiritual meaning. Your religion is your structured belief system, while spirituality is the unquenchable thirst for meaning in your life that leads you to become more committed to life. The psychologist, Ken Wilber writes that spirituality is the force that weaves together all aspects of the person, all people, and nature

When you and I move from suffering to the realization that we will always be ourselves and we can always depend upon ourselves, we will have the courage to become our spiritual selves through self-trust and self-love. You will reach within yourself to accept, love, and value whatever you find there. Your self-acceptance then turns into self-reliance. When people have a serious illness, they might express it as one of my research participants did, "No matter what my disease does or what the world brings, I can count on me."

Gayle

Gayle is young woman, who had always been overshadowed by her high achieving family. She never felt that she was as good or as smart as her parents or her sister. But since her HIV diagnosis, she has grown so much in her ability to be spiritual. In describing how she now manages difficult problems she said,

> I have really surprised myself in the way I have learned to handle a situation. I couldn't have done it a few years ago. I feel really good about it. Something will happen, and I'm hurt inside. Then I go, "Wait, why am I feeling this vulnerable? I need to back up and see where I should be, what can I do for me." I came home one day and went, "ah…(sigh), this is one of the hardest days I have ever had in a long time, but I am here at the end of it and I am still me, and I still have grace and integrity. That's what it's been about to have this spirit.

So an important component of your spirituality is when you move from suffering to the realization that you have yourself, that you like yourself, and that you will always be yourself, no matter what happens. This realization is most powerful, and will stay with you to support and comfort always, even on the day you die.

John

This latter statement was brought home to me as I interviewed John, a 39 year old hospice worker who had been such an inspiration in my life, as I had worked with him over the years to care for persons dying of AIDS. He was very ill. His hospice worker told me that John would be dead in less than a week. I worried about intruding on him, taking up his precious time in his few remaining days. But he insisted that he wanted to be part of my research study. He was so close to dying that he was having out of body experiences that are pretty common in people who are near death. He said to me:

> I fly over my bed at night and look at myself. I just have the feeling that I am not in my body. I don't think I have ever traveled far. Mostly what I see is my body, and I'm above it. It's a real warm feeling. Don't feel I have a lot hanging over my shoulders anymore. I feel like I have a peaceful existence. I don't have a lot of regrets. I think that death is going to be an okay experience. I can have it pretty much any way I want. I don't think it will be a horrible emotional thing. For the most part I understand that when its time, it's time. I have gotten a lot of comfort from being around other people who were dying. I think just liking myself is an important part of how it's going to be. I don't feel fear anymore. I feel that death is a natural part of life. It's okay. We are all going to be together and be taken care of. I really like myself and I will always be myself.

When you accept that there is a purpose to your life and to everything that happens in your life, you allow a turn around in the meaning of your illness, from a tragic happening that was visited on you like an ancient plague, to a life event that has function and meaning. For ill people, the act of searching for answers in an atmosphere of love and acceptance frees them to look at the meaning of both their life and their illness in a different way, as they begin to accept themselves and let go of emotions that have had a negative effect on their self esteem. When we grasp that we are wonderful creations just the way we are – as one man put it, "When I stopped beating myself up and started seeing myself as perfectly created for what I have to do," is when we began to feel astonished at the enormity of our growing spiritual authenticity. The rush of happiness that comes from the realization that we have transcended our narrow purposes, and that peace and love are real possibilities in our relationships, takes us into a new space with ourselves and others.

Jim

Jim had always been very bitter about his life growing up in a family in which he did not feel loved. He suffered harsh treatment from his minister father from childhood to the present because Jim was gay. In so many ways, he had not lived up to his expectations for himself, and suffered from lingering anger at his family. He had cut himself off from close relationships in an attempt at self-protection. When I interviewed him about how his illness had changed his outlook on himself and others, he said,

> I finally understood that the soul that inhabited Jesus had to have been the same soul that inhabited Buddha, Mohammed, and all the people of the world, including my father. I started seeing the connectedness of everything and everyone.

After having this revelation, Jim called his father and asked to see him. At the end of their visit, Jim's father put his arms around him and said, "You are my son and I have always loved you. I am sorry for the way I did not show it all these years." Jim's life has changed from his old guarded and fearful existence to a close, thoughtful, and satisfying world in which he can participate as a full human being and be member of a family for the first time in years.

Dr. Daniel Helminiak has spent a great deal of his professional life formulating the meaning of spirituality. When he was a Catholic priest, and then later as a student in his PhD program in psychology, he laid out the meaning of the human spirit from a secular point of view. According to him, our spirituality evolves as we become our authentic selves. You will know you are living an authentic life when you are follow the four principles set down by the theologian, Lonergan: Be attentive, be intelligent, be reasonable, and be responsible. All these taken together form a picture of a person who is open to experience and committed to the welfare of all that surrounds. In fact, taking authenticity to be the foundation of spirituality, Helminiak says that it is determined by self-awareness and it is experienced as being open to all there is to be known and loved. To be that open would be quite a turnaround for most of us, who lead our lives in very protected ways, guarding ourselves from strong emotions; shielding ourselves from the full life that we could live if we were openly experiencing it.

Ted

Ted was a loner. Although he had always wanted a close relationship, he had never accepted anyone into his life. After living with HIV for several years, Ted was still healthy, but one day at his doctor's office, he met Ben, who was very ill and close to dying. For some reason, Ted was moved by Ben's illness and the fact that Ben had nobody to care for him. He invited Ben into his home on a temporary basis, but ended up caring for him until he died. During Ted's interview, he said,

> My definition of spirituality has become more about understanding my commitments to other people. My meaning in life has changed. I was a survivor before. I had that nice Irish view that life was something to be gotten through. I got to grow beyond that.

Robert Frost, in his poem at John F. Kennedy's inauguration, issued the same sentiments when he warned us about the living our lives in isolation from others.

> *Something we were withholding made us weak,*
> *Until we discovered it was ourselves.*
> *We were withholding from our land of living.*

So, your spirituality is a culmination of your investments in your own life and the lives of others. It is about healing, openness, and authenticity. Ken Wilber, the renowned psychologist talks about Hell as being the separate self. In illness, we are first tempted to fall into the yawning pit of more isolation as we sniff in self-pity over our plight. We can become stuck finding the answer to the questions of "Why me? What have I done to deserve this?" Or we can grasp the opportunity to embrace life, and we can use these same questions to start on a simple pursuit in search of the answers to greater questions of what we have to learn from fear, pain, and debilitation that will make us better able to be ourselves, trust ourselves, and live the life we came to live.

Paradoxically we find life by finding ourselves. Ken Wilber's advice is to, "Look within until within becomes beyond." This suggests that your spiritual awaking means that you finally acquire the knowledge, in a way in which you are totally convinced, that the entire world is all made of the same stuff as is inside you. So many of my patients and research informants have learned the valuable lesson that when you go inside, you see that there is no self apart from the world. When you discover the divine within you - the divine that is there waiting for your discovery - you will see this same divine mirrored in the external world around you.

Self love is not self absorption. All love is learned from love of yourself, yet it is something that we are never taught. I assure you that I was never taught self-love in Sunday school where all I learned about was my sins. While most of us are never taught about self-love, we have all had experiences that have eroded self-love. Two important ones are rejection by revered others, and failure to meet the goals that others hold for us when we are children.

The educational philosopher, Noddings, teaches that caring for others always begins with the feeling of how it was to be cared for - through the memory of our past experiences in which someone cared for us. So self-caring is experienced as remembered emotions – the warm, comforting feelings we had, especially when growing up, that were our responses to care. An important link to self-love then, is to regain, through meditation or reflection, those times when you have felt loved and cared for. You will learn through accessing these memories that love of yourself has never been an option in your life, it is a complete necessity.

In Chapters 6, and 7, and 8 I have given you the tools to begin looking within - prayer, meditation, and imaging. In deep meditation, ask yourself and your spirit guide for assistance in your efforts to go deeply toward your path of self-discovery. Examine your own mind and conscience to remember whom you need to forgive, whom you need to give to, and whom you need to love more dearly. As you hear the answers to these questions, relax and as one of my research informants put it, "Learn to go where life takes you." Learn to live your beliefs, for it is in learning to live a life that you are led to become the spiritual person you want to be. Your words and labels explain the phenomenon, but words will not show the way. Experiences do that for you. Most important, and write this in your diary if you need to: *Your spirituality will foreground a focus on your strengths, not your faults.* You are done with beating yourself up. As you reach for meaning, you will find that the real meaning of your life involves what you are now discovering for yourself about your strength. To summarize it all, then, spirituality means learning to:

- Trust, love, and rely on yourself and others.
- See the significance of your own strength.
- Give all that you have.
- Forgive yourself and others.
- Accept meaning in your life in whatever form it comes.

THE
THIRD
CHALLENGE:

Focusing Your Attention On What Your
Body Needs To Heal

There is a mountain of research on the role of nutrition and exercise in promoting health, preventing illness, and healing disease. In this section you will learn what to eat and what nutrients to add to your diet that will put your body in the best position to cure itself. I will tell you about the nutritional regime that I have adhered to for the past 25 years, and that I believe saved my life.

Then I will help you to understand why exercise is vitally significant to your survival from illness. The importance of exercise cannot be overstated. Most of us know that we should exercise more than we do, but a great many factors conspire to keep us sedentary. So I will show you how you can overcome some of the inertia that we all feel when trying to adopt a new health practice.

Chapter 10

Nutrition: Diet And Vitamins

I am not a nutritionist, but I have been a student of nutrition, starting more than 25 years ago when I began to search frantically for a way to cure myself from cancer. Surprisingly the regimen that I put myself on then has been supported remarkably by research, even though at the time I ferreted out the evidence, it was vague, slim, and hard to access. Over the years I have added some things and subtracted others, but mostly, the advice I got then; advice was considered "far out" and weird, has been held up over the years, and is part of what a large number of experts now believe.

In the fast food paradise in which we live, it is easy to go around acting as though there are no costs to eating huge amounts of awful food. An astonishing two out of three Americans are overweight or obese. It is hard to believe that anyone would honestly believe that the average American diet is healthy, so a lot of people are probably looking for a way to change this harmful pattern. The evidence of mounting weight and sluggish metabolism are two of the early consequences of slogging through a daily diet that lacks the essential vitamins and minerals that your body needs to work properly. If poor nutrition is damaging to those who are not yet ill, think how it could be fatal for anyone with a life threatening diagnosis.

My philosophy is that you can eat almost any kind of food, even foods that are not all that good for you, if you eat small amounts and only occasionally. So how about right now resolving to follow a healthful nutritional plan for a month with the promise to yourself that if you wish, you can spend a day eating some of the things you miss. But be warned that this may not turn out to be the way that you will end up rewarding yourself. The fast foods that you have been eating are greatly addicting, and when you get accustomed to a healthier diet, you will no longer crave them. You will still enjoy some, but may never regain the enjoyment you used to get from your old standbys.

I believe that my diet and nutritional supplements have contributed greatly to my 25 year survival from cancer in the face of a very poor prognosis. There were other things of course, described in other chapters, but when someone consults me for advice after a serious diagnosis, the nutritional plan that I present in this chapter is the first thing that I go over with them. Antioxidant vitamins are so vital to saving lives that I treat nutritional interventions as emergency care.

I routinely tell people to check with their health providers about diets, although some may have had very little, if any, training in nutrition beyond the foods that ameliorate symptoms that cause disease. For example, you may have been advised to decrease fat and salt in order to lower cholesterol and blood pressure. You may be advised to take certain vitamins after a heart attack to lower your chance of having another one, and so on. This information is important, but because it is dietary advice that focuses on symptoms and lab findings it is not aimed at improvement in overall health. A diet that contains total nutrition is often the last thing any health professional will talk with you about. Some patients have told me that a physician or other clinician has actively discouraged them from taking vitamin supplements based upon the idea that we should get all of what our body needs from food. Fortunately, the professionals who tender such unscientific myths to ill people are rapidly disappearing from the medical scene. I wonder where they think most people can even buy the food that would contain all the nutrients that are needed by a person who is healthy, much less one who is ill or trying to cope with the onslaughts of powerful medical treatments being used to treat their disease. In my years of working with people who have a serious illness, I have found that when physicians get sick, they will themselves often turn to healing practices that are outside their own training as doctors.

Joan

Joan is a 30 year old family practice physician who got a copy of my survivor's guide from a nurse in her practice after her surgery for breast cancer. Joan discovered her cancer while pregnant. As a physician she knew very well the dismal implications of what they had found in staging the extent of her disease. She knew that I had lived a long time after my diagnosis, with a worse prognosis then hers, and was impressed with my results. She called me and asked if I would go over my nutritional recommendations with her and James, her husband. They came to my house with their newborn baby who slept peacefully on a pallet on the floor, cuddled with my large, gentle cat, Max, while we talked about diet and supplements.

Joan was the breadwinner in her family. She needed to regain her health as quickly as possible and to be able to work while she was undergoing treatment. I gave her a list of what supplements to buy and showed her how to set up a "vitamin box," a plastic box with many small compartments that would contain all the pills she needed for several days. Additionally, I told her that traditionally in this country there has been very little interest in research on antioxidants, and certainly none by the pharmaceutical companies who do most of the drug research in the United States. In most cases the evidence comes from research and clinical practice conducted in European countries like France, Germany, Russia, and the United Kingdom, whose evidence is based upon both clinical trials and anecdotal information. Thankfully, I could also assure her that what I recommend is not harmful. Joan followed my advice. The last I heard, Joan was doing very well, having accepted a position with an organization that delivers health care to impoverished people in other countries.

Sources For Supplements

Over the years I have become quite adept at sifting though evidence and hype, and especially at sorting out which companies push their money-making schemes onto the gullible public from those that manufacture good products at reasonable prices. There are a great number of reliable manufactures, and many of them can be found on the Internet. If you have a health food store in your community, talk to the vitamin buyers and find out what they recommend from the list that you bring in.

I do not buy supplements from companies that sound like they are promoting pyramid schemes. There are a number of reasons for this decision, and the biggest two are cost and quality. For most that I have investigated, the hype is huge, the research is vague, and recommendations are cast from testimonials of "satisfied users." Lastly, because a company has hired a medical doctor to front for the company's research agenda does not make it legitimate. These spokespersons can sound very erudite, while speaking on behalf of a product that is overpriced and has questionable effectiveness.

Resources For Nutritional Information

There are some excellent books for the layperson. I regularly visit the self-help section in bookstores and I read reviews of new books in the journals I subscribe to. There are thousands of books and internet sites on nutrition. Many are based up nothing except the author's hair brained idea, such as "How I cured my cancer with wheat germ and water." You do have to be very, very careful in this field, so let your good sense lead the way.

The best nutrition book for the public that I have ever read is by Shari Lieberman and Nancy Bruning, *The Real Vitamin & Mineral Book*. This book has been described in the *Townsend Letter,* as the gold standard for nutritional supplement guides. The authors teach you about nutrition, recommend specific supplements, cite the applicable research that support their recommendations, and go over which foods are high in each nutrient.

If you have Internet access, I urge you to explore the vast sources of information contained there. The *National Center for Complementary Medicine* within *The National Institutes of Health (NIH)* has a website devoted to information on current and past studies at www.nccam.nih.gov. If you don't know what site you want, just enter the name of the supplement or the name of the physical condition you want to address. I just entered a search for Cranberry Juice for a friend with a bladder infection. I got dozens of excellent hits, one of which was from NIH

Nutritional Recommendations

These recommendations are very basic, yet in a modern world you may have trouble living by them at first. I do not think anyone has to be a perfectionist. You are not going to drop dead if you eat some dessert or have a slice of white bread. In my own life I try to eat in as healthy a way as possible, but I am definitely not obsessive about it. I occasionally use artificial sweeteners, although I try to limit them. I cook in microwave ovens. I have never read any convincing evidence of any harm they do if used correctly. You will hear or read about many such issues and will have to decide how to handle them for yourself. All my nutritional recommendations should be viewed as guidelines that you can use to set dietary goals that you will strive to achieve. First, here is the simple advice:

> **Decrease**: Alcohol, fats from animal protein, lard and other fats added to baked goods, charred food, pickled food, white flour, white rice, and sugar.

> **Increase**: All vegetables, fruits, cruciferous vegetables, whole grains, healthy fats, and healthy sources of protein.

Protein – Eggs, Dairy, Meat, Fish And Fowl

A sufficient amount of protein is very necessary for healing and for maintaining health. No matter what kind of diet you eat, you should be getting at least five servings of a complete protein every day. This is very difficult for many people on a vegetarian diet, especially those who do not eat eggs or dairy products, or who do not combine vegetables, such as beans, rice, and corn, that when eaten together, form a complete protein.

When I was studying acupuncture I examined the dietary intake of a vegetarian patient who ate a lot of her meals in restaurants. I discovered that she got so little protein that I felt she was fortunate to be alive at all. She had been losing energy and, I believe that the neurological symptom for which she was being treated was becoming much worse as a function of her diet low in protein. Many experts believe that a vegetarian diet is useful and healthful. A lot of the information on vegetarianism in our country has been collected from vegetarian Seventh Day Adventists and others who do not eat meat for religious reasons. Since both religious and non-religious vegetarians tend to have excellent health habits, such as limiting alcohol and not smoking, the reasons for the positive health findings from diet cannot be determined by reviewing vegetarian health outcomes. So while we think that vegetarianism is healthy, we do not really know for sure. I am not a vegetarian, although I was for many years. But I gradually went back to including some meat, chicken, and fish, because I came to believe that eating only vegetables was not healthy for me. Some people do not do well on a vegetarian diet, while others seem to thrive on it. A diet with too little protein has been implicated as one of the primary causes of lowered immunity. I urge you to add up your protein sources to make sure you are getting about 50gms/day.

Antioxidants

Vitamins support your growth and development and are factors in prevention, healing, and reversing disease processes. The antioxidant effect on the body is an important purpose of vitamins that has been uncovered within the last 15 years. Research has shown that antioxidants buffer and protect. Whether you are getting them through your diet or as supplements to your diet, antioxidants act as scavengers on free radicals, thus preventing or reversing the damage to DNA, membranes and tissues that is the cause of most diseases. Free radicals are toxic molecules that wage war on healthy tissues as we breathe polluted air or digest our food.

Some scientists have portrayed all deterioration of the body, whether of disease, aging, or wearing down, as a battle between the bad guys, *free radicals*, which corrode and destroy, and the saviors, *antioxidants*, which absorb the unwanted extra electron, putting an end to its rampage of destruction. Thus antioxidants prevent cell damage, reverse the damage caused by disease, and help you to survive and thrive after a life threatening diagnosis.

Very little was known about antioxidants when I was diagnosed 25 years ago. Most people laughed at Linus Pauling's pronouncements about vitamin C. It is true that not all of Pauling's theoretical reasoning was accurate. Pauling was a Nobel Laureate chemist who devoted a number of years to the scientific study of vitamin C, and I honestly believe that his work saved my life. After reading his research, I started myself on humongous doses of vitamin C, around 50 to 60 grams a day. I still take 8 - 10 grams a day. Vitamin C is one of the most fundamental antioxidants – most of us go through a great deal of it as we cope with many types of pollutants in the air, food and water. The more toxic substances we encounter, the more C we need. Smokers, for example may need ten times as much as non-smokers. Because we now have an array of antioxidants, each with a little different impact on the body, we do not have to rely on such huge doses of vitamin C alone, as I did then.

As long as 18 years ago, Pauling detected that vitamin C was antiviral. It appears that he did not know why this was so, but from his own investigations on health he laid out a vitamin regimen that I started on and am still taking. In addition to vitamin C, he was one of the first to recommend trace minerals and the B vitamins: folic acid, vitamin B12 and B6. Perhaps this kind of forward thinking is why Dr. Linus Pauling was awarded not one, but two Nobel Prizes. For everyone living, I recommend vitamin C, but for people with cancer, HIV, and heart disease, I believe that it is absolutely essential. It is one of the general antioxidants that seem to affect positively the tissues in every part of the body.

Recommendations In A Nutshell

Diet

The following foods are a very important source of antioxidants. They are essential for the health of all people, but they are most vital for persons recovering from illness, fighting off disease, recovering from surgery, or taking invasive chemical or radiation treatments for cancer.

Fruits: Add a lot of these to your diet

Eat regularly those fruits that are purple or dark in color. So for example when you have a choice, eat **purple grapes**, not green grapes. Dark fruits are high in the antioxidant quercetin and contain the powerful free radical scavengers, procyanidins. Procyanidins are very complex molecules that release powerful antioxidants. The fat in **avocados** is the type that is good for you. They are very rich in the antioxidant glutathione. **Citrus fruits** (whole fruit, not juice), especially orange and grapefruit are high in every anti-cancer antioxidant. Dark or **purple berries** are loaded with antioxidants and vitamin C. They are also high in fiber, which contributes to bowel health and weight loss.

Vegetables: All vegetables are healthy. I have selected some that are essential.

Some of these vegetables are not the best tasting things in the world, but hold your nose until you acquire a taste for them. Eat as much as you can of the following vegetables because they are very high in antioxidants and minerals: **broccoli, brussels sprouts**, and **cabbage** are the cruciferous vegetables that have been noted in hundreds of research studies to protect against cancer. **carrots** are important because they contain alpha and beta carotene. Cooked **tomatoes** also contain carotenoids that protect against free radicals that cause some types of cancer (breast and prostate cancer have been documented in the research) and cardiovascular disease. Apparently cooking tomatoes is what brings out lycopene, a very stable compound that survives a lot of food processing, and is responsible for many health benefits, including lowering the risk of major types of cancer and possibly heart disease. Round out your food plan with a salad made with **lettuce, spinach, sprouts, mushrooms, radishes, green beans, cucumbers, nuts,** and anything else you can find in the fresh foods section of the grocery store. Your body will appreciate the fiber, potassium, and vitamins contained in this raw medley. You will also benefit from the fiber in **onions** and **garlic.** Both are also full of the antioxidant, allium. Eat at least 3 garlic cloves a day. Allium takes awhile to synthesize after these vegetables are cut or smashed. Heat will destroy it if you throw them into the pan right away. Wait about 5 minutes after chopping onions or garlic before you cook them. Allium is most important for decreasing cancer risk and lowering cholesterol. If the smell of garlic and onions bothers your friends, they should eat some too so they won't be able to smell it.

And, finally, decrease white rice, white pasta and potatoes and go for the whole grains which are full of fiber and vitamins. These changes may not be easy at first. Decreasing potatoes, white rice, and white pasta made my stomach wonder if my throat had been cut. I still long for a softly baked potato, skin crusty and brown, with butter and sour cream dripping all over it - and dished up with a giant rare steak, served with ranch dressing poured over a crisp salad. I mention this to remind you that nothing is forbidden, just to be limited to those occasions when you simply have to have them or else you feel you will die

Tea: A life giving drink.

Use green or black tea, and drink 3 to 4 cups a day. It is full of antioxidants. Most of the research has been focused on green tea, but other forms are equally healthful. The type of alertness that green tea produces has been called, "alert relaxation," because it boosts alpha waves that allow you to focus and be calm without jangling the nerves. It reduces the risk of colorectal and pancreatic cancer. It is antioxidant and diuretic. It has been shown to inhibit cancer and platelet aggregation, and lower cholesterol. I figured that tea had arrived after I learned that the cancer center at MD Anderson was promoting its own brand of green tea extract capsules.

Soybean Foods: For better or for worse.

Soy contains many antioxidants that have immuno-potentiating benefits, but I recommended a daily portion of no more than 2-4 ounces. More recent investigation has warned against taking too much soy, because of its depressing effect on the thyroid gland. *The Townsend Letter* has presented a number of debates on the use of soy, some authors claiming that it is not healthful at all, while others arguing that while too much may be harmful; the right amount is very beneficial. Experts agree that loading up on soy powder or soy drinks is a bad idea. Eat soy like the Asians do, in tofu and miso. I also caution you about the use of soybean oil. The question is not entirely settled, but there is some evidence that it may not be as healthful for use in low fat diets as we have always thought. For the sides of the debate on this issue see *The Good Fat Cookbook*, which you can find in the reference list.

Olive Oil: Life giving fat.

Cook with olive oil and use it in salads. A recent study showed that women who ate pizza twice a week had lower rates of colon cancer. This difference was attributed solely to the fact that pizza contains tomatoes and olive oil. You don't have to eat pizza to get tomatoes and olive oil. If you want to use butter for frying, I suggest that you use a mixture of half butter and half olive oil. Honestly, I don't think butter is the worst thing you can eat.

Chocolate: Food of the gods.

Chocolate has been called the "healing food of the gods," because it has been used in many traditional cultures for healing. The cacao bean is considered a sacred object in some indigenous cultures. I think that I too, consider it a sacred object. Dark chocolate contains polyphenol antioxidants. Be judicious of course in how much you consume of this sweet food. You should not gobble it down as often as you may be tempted to do because it has too much fat and sugar.

Vitamin And Mineral Supplements

The following vitamins and minerals support health of the entire body, and are to accompany a healthy diet, not replace it. That is why they are called "supplements," not "diets." You need more of certain supplements not only to support health, but also as protection from the assaults on your body from medications, radiation and surgery.

Multivitamin with minerals: Take daily or 2 times daily (depending on strength of the vitamin). Taking this will insure that you have at least the minimum of most of the essential vitamins and minerals.

Dry E or water soluble E: Take 400 IU, including what is in the multivitamin. Vitamin E is a powerful antioxidant and cancer fighter. If you are a smoker or have a low platelet count, do not take large amounts of E.

Vitamin C as Powered Sodium or Calcium Ascorbate or Ascorbic Acid: Take 8 to 12 grams per day in divided doses. Vitamin C has been shown to reduce the side effects of chemotherapy and other treatments for cancer. It also increases resistance to a number of diseases, including cancer and cardiovascular disease. Sodium ascorbate was the form of vitamin C tested in Pauling and Cameron's studies that provided complete remission in many patients with terminal cancer. I recommend all forms to you. I mix them equally so that I get the benefits of both the ascorbates and ascorbic acid, and I find that when mixed each makes the other taste better. The ascorbates are easier on the digestion than the less expensive ascorbic acid. Take the dosage up to bowel tolerance – cut back if you develop diarrhea or excessive gas. Divide the total amount into 2- 3 doses to increase absorption and prevent diarrhea. You may take ester C tablets instead if you are traveling or want to carry them around with you. You may take small amounts every few hours, if you wish, but do not take large doses on an empty stomach, as this could cause diarrhea.

Studies of persons with cancer, particularly lung cancer, show that they are usually very deficient in this vitamin and may be able to supplement very large amounts before showing signs of bowel intolerance. When I was in chemotherapy and radiation, I took as high as 50 grams a day with no bowel disturbance at all. Now, I can only tolerate 8-10 grams. If you are bothered by embarrassing production of gas from vitamin C, and cutting back the dose does not relieve it, try taking the herb, ginger. You can buy it in the produce section of the grocery store. Cut it up and use it in cooking or make ginger tea by pouring boiling water over cut up thin slices.

Vitamin B12: Take 500 - 1000 mcg per day in divided doses. Current research shows that even among persons who lack the intrinsic factor needed to metabolize oral vitamin B12, some of the vitamin in large oral doses will be absorbed in the stomach. Persons who have auto immune diseases or who are over 50 should take the higher dose.

Folic Acid: Take 1000 mcg one time a day (*Important*: do not supplement folic acid unless you are also supplementing vitamin B12). Along with vitamin B12, folic acid helps to lower homocysteine levels. There is current debate about the relationship between homocysteine and heart disease. No conclusive scientific test has settled the question, but since it does no harm, I recommend we continue the supplementation.

Vitamin D: Take 800-1200 IU daily. Vitamin D is also a hormone because humans manufacture this vitamin in the skin when exposed directly to the sun. But sun exposure is limited in certain climates and seasons. The scientific community has recently evaluated the role of vitamin D in prevention of breast, colon, and prostate cancer, autoimmune diseases, and heart disease. Its effect appears to underlie a great many human metabolic process, not just formation of bone. Studies are ongoing, but I predict that this vitamin will assume a very prominent role in health maintenance and disease prevention in the future. Even high doses appear to be safe. Check your label to make sure you are getting vitamin D as D3 or cholecalciferol.

Omega 3 Essential Fatty Acids (EFA): Take as fish oil or flax seed oil. There is no established optimum intake for EFAs. Omega 3 EFAs are found in cold water fish, such as tuna and salmon. Try to eat this type of fish once a week and also supplement daily with fish or flax oil, (1000 mg/day) which is relatively inexpensive and very effective. EFA acts as a natural blood thinner which is more effective than aspirin. It lowers blood pressure, cholesterol, and triglycerides. The EFA found in fish oil also inhibits cancer growth. Another EFA, borage oil has an important use in reducing inflammation and inhibiting cancer.

Selenium: Take 50 -200 mcg one time a day for cancer and heart disease prevention.

Zinc: Take 15- 30 mg one time a day. Zinc is protective of the liver, especially if you are receiving chemotherapy or other medications that may act as toxins to the liver.

Calcium and Magnesium: Take 500 to 1500 mg Calcium and 250 to 750 mg magnesium in 2 divided doses. Note: I have found one supplement that contains the correct doses of all the minerals and trace minerals in the correct amounts: *Nature's Life Vegetarian Mega-Minerals*. It saves both time and money to take them all in this one pill.

Co-enzyme Q-10: Take 30-150 mg a day. We are learning more about the antioxidant properties of this enzyme every year for cancer and heart disease. In fact the heart muscle contains a high amount of co-Q. Because co-Q has such an affinity for heart tissue, an abundant food source is in animal hearts. Lieberman and Bruning discuss in detail the Japanese research that has shown a beneficial impact on congestive heart disease and arrhythmias. If you have gum disease, which often accompanies treatments for cancer that lower immunity, Co-Q will retard this disease. When I started taking it as an anticancer enzyme about 10 years ago, I found that my gum disease, which was so severe that I was about to lose all my teeth, cleared up.

Oligomeric Procyanidins (OPC) - Grape Seed Extract: Take .5 to .8 mg. per pound of body weight. Grape seed extract is an antioxidant that is many times more powerful than vitamin E. It is a very effective immune system stimulator and free radical scavenger. There is some evidence that supports the use of grape seed in tumor inhibition. This is based on animal results and from anecdotal evidence from many sources that supports the use of OPC antioxidants such as grape seed in cancer and HIV. Many other fruits and vegetables, such as cranberry juice also contain procyanidins. A word of caution about taking to much of this antioxidant concerns its blood thinning action, especially if you are taking anti-clotting prescription medications or aspirin.

Dehydroepiandrosterone (DHEA): If you are over 55-60, you might ask your doctor about supplementing DHEA. It is being shown to be a cancer fighter. Because it is an estrogen and testosterone precursor (activates the synthesis of these hormones in the body) it also lessens symptoms of menopause in women, and supports better testosterone levels in aging men. The handful of studies done on DHEA has supported claims that it restores memory, reduces body fat, and fights cancer and heart disease. A consistently positive outcome of trials in older individuals is a notable increase in one's optimism and outlook on life. Women with estrogen sensitive breast tumors can take DHEA. It actually could reduce the risk of a recurrence because it takes up the estrogen receptor sites in the breast, thus preventing estrogen from gaining access there and activating breast tumor growth. Take 10-15 mg, and give it a few months to work. Some patients in clinical trials felt the effects right away, but for others, the impact was much slower. Men seem to have few problems with DHEA and can handle a higher dose, but some women will develop receding hair (male pattern baldness), facial hair, and lowering of voice. These symptoms will disappear when you reduce the dose to what I have recommended above.

Final warning: Many oncologists give strong advice not to take antioxidant supplements with chemotherapy. This warning appears to be based on one animal study and theoretical reasoning. In all but a few cases, there is a huge benefit, although there are a few chemotherapeutic drugs in which antioxidants may interfere. There have been many articles showing an overwhelming benefit for concurrent cytoxic treatment and antioxidant therapies. To obtain a summary of all the arguments and the couple of exceptions to my advice, see Moss, RW. *The Concurrent use of antioxidants and cytoxic cancer treatment:* www.cancerdecisions.com/denmark2001.html.

Further reading and additional consultation is a requirement for survivors who want to follow the advice contained in this section of the book. My personal recommendations for diet and supplements are based upon my own opinions garnered from a continuous and relentless effort toward self education that has taken place over a period of more than 25 years. In turning over these recommendations to you, I have been very conscientious in adhering to safety in both dosage and types of nutrients. I left out all things that may present a potential harm, even when I was very sure they would not do so. I have also taken pains to let you know when there is controversy surrounding the use of a supplement. But please begin your own health education. Sometimes the latest findings that are presented as news headlines will lead you astray. Personally I rarely pay heed to much of the information from the newspaper regarding supplementation of vitamins, because I have learned that some researchers conduct studies that use inappropriately small doses, they announce their findings before their studies are conclusive, and they have not built upon the data from other countries. I will read for example that there has been no scientific research on a certain vitamin or herb when I personally know about dozens of scientifically rigorous trials. The two sources that follow will help you to evaluate the headline pronouncements that you hear on radio and television and read in newspapers and magazines.

The Townsend Letter: A great deal of the information spread throughout this chapter has been influenced by what I have read in this journal. So much of what I believe about nutrition and fitness has been confirmed and even formed by the regularly appearing columns and articles about the latest findings on alternative and complementary health care. Much of the good information that this journal brings forward is found lurking in the pages of nutritional journals that I would never read. I recommend it to you as one way of keeping up with latest findings in health and nutrition. Phone: 360/385-6021; Website: www.townsendletter.com.

National Center for Complementary and Alternative Medicine: This center, which is part of the National Institutes of Health, is charged with funding quality studies that evaluate alternative medical practices. You can access this agency through their Website, www.nccam.nih.gov. It provides health information and ways to access information about specific practices and supplements.

Chapter 11

Get Moving: The Importance Of Physical Activity

The evidence that supports the health benefits of exercise is overwhelming and convincing to scientists and health providers. Research shows that physical activity will prevent illness that you are at risk for and will help to cure whatever ails you – serious physical illness, emotional problems, and obesity. According to the U.S. Preventive Services Task Force, regular physical activity prevents illness and death from a great number of diseases, such as diabetes and cardiovascular disease. And, these benefits can be achieved with very modest and achievable levels, such as walking or bicycling 30 minutes a day for most days of the week.

The evidence for all the gains in health from exercise is so persuasive that virtually no one disputes them. Paradoxically, while evidence has piled up about the benefits of being active, sedentary and obese adults have become the norm. Now if you have any reason at all to think that it might be harmful to get out of the chair and work up to a half-hour walking program, check with your physician or other health provider. Chances are enormous that there will be no reason at all why you cannot engage in physical activity that is right for your health and age.

Walking: Most of us can walk for exercise because it requires no real training and no equipment except good walking shoes. Into the bargain, it is not hard to build up to the recommended level. You don't even have to do it every single day, only around 4 times a week. If you are a beginner, you need to start at a slow pace, say one mile in 20 to 30 minutes. After you begin to adjust to lower levels of exercise increasing your speed and distance will bring even greater benefits to physical and mental health. But know that even at lower levels you are doing your body a great favor, and it will thank you.

Slow walking is usually very safe, but even so, you need to take some precautions in advance. Almost all exercise injuries can be accounted for by excessive speed, walking too fast uphill, exceeding your level of conditioning, not preparing your body for its workout, or not wearing shoes with good support. So wear good walking shoes and try to warm up with some stretching exercises

Before a workout, stretch all your joints by going through a range of motion with each joint. If you are confused about how to do this, you may need to consult with a knowledgeable friend, a trainer, or a book. An important warning about stretching is not to bounce. Do a slow and steady stretch for each joint in your body, taking each joint to its fullest range that is comfortable. Begin your walk slowly for a few minutes to give your muscles a chance to warm up, and then increase your speed. The last 5 minutes of any exercise period is known as the cool down. Walk at a slower speed. Then end with a little more stretching. It is as easy as pie.

Other Exercise: So many forms of physical activity are beneficial, among them biking, swimming, active sports, climbing stairs, gardening, lifting, and walking while you are engaged in chores like shopping, and so on. The idea is to get moving. All these activities bring needed oxygen to the mitochondria of the muscles, which improves blood flow to the muscles, and results in increased oxygenation of tissues. Activity promotes general circulation of blood. The benefits are enormous to your cardiovascular system and your brain as well as to every organ in your body. To help you, there are many Internet sites devoted to exercise. Some of them are government sponsored sites. Simply key in the word, "Exercise" and go on an exciting exploration and get a lot of free advice.

Traditions From The East

Yoga: I have done yoga for many years, even before it was so popular. Yoga is concerned with the health of the entire body – physical, mental, and spiritual. Most notable is its effect on toning up the whole body, and delaying aging. It provides relaxation benefits that last long after a session. The various poses or *asanas* are based upon ancient knowledge that over the centuries has dealt with ways to affect positively the joints, muscles, circulation, and internal organs. Yoga has become such a craze that it is not difficult to find a class in almost any health club. Search the free newspapers that are on the stands at the supermarket for ads for community classes. If all else fails, buy a paper back book that will take you through lessons on breathing and poses.

Tai Chi: When I lived in San Francisco, I would notice the older Chinese men and women in Golden Gate Park doing Tai Chi. The meditative and peaceful effects of their ritual were so apparent to any observer. Some of these elders were in their 90th to 100th decade, but were so coordinated and flexible. It turns out that Tai Chi does have tremendous health outcomes and indeed it reverses and prevents aging of the body and mind. It increases blood circulation, lowers blood pressure, increases healing from infection and disease, and promotes flexibility in joints and muscles.

The Tibetan Five Rites: Many years ago I picked up a small book by a man named Peter Kelder called, *The Ancient Secret of the Fountain of Youth.* The practices he recommended quickly developed into an almost cult following. The five rites have been circulated through Kelder's book, the internet, and word of mouth for many years. I have done these exercises for the last 10 years and have taught many others to do them. Like me, the people I have passed them on to, have experienced the anti-aging outcomes promised in the book. They consist of five exercises that are performed 21 times each, after building up slowly. The instantaneous effect that people feel, starting the first time they perform them is in the form of an amazing burst of energy and feeling of well being immediately after doing them. This exuberant feeling keeps people doing them. They do not take a very much time, especially considering the remarkable healing effects they have on the body, mind, and spirit. Several Internet sites can instruct you on how to do the five rites.

Overcoming Resistance To Anything New

When you are adopting a new routine it takes a long time before it feels natural. At first, it will not fit in with the rest of your life. Over time you can make all the many adjustments that allow an activity to be just a part of what you do every day, instead of something you are adding reluctantly onto everything else. After a short time, say three months, of doing exercise every day, if you skip it you will feel like something important is missing in your day. So a vital key to success is finding a way to continue your exercises until it becomes part of what you look forward to every day - the type of necessity that you would never think of skipping.

With regular exercise, life takes on a new flavor and a new color. You start your exercise each day with a powerful exuberance, as you look forward to the experience of flexing your muscles and getting into a zone of movement. Even though you may not look like a model, you will start to feel that you are at your fighting weight, and at a level of fitness that makes everything you do during the day easier. These specific steps will get you started on your new routine.

Step 1. Establish your reasons for exercising. You surely know that exercise holds vast life giving benefits for you, physically and mentally. Try now to think of some specific reasons that apply to your particular situation. Do you want to live longer, look and feel better, decrease weight, firm up, lower blood pressure, fight cancer, lower stress, sleep better, or combat depression? Do you want to lower your chances of getting diabetes, contracting virtually all diseases, or delay or retard the progression of a number of diseases, such as diabetes or Alzheimer's? These are only a few of the effects of exercise. So, right now, stop and write down your reasons, so that you can look at them every day. When other reasons emerge, add them.

Step 2. Establish goals for exercising. One of the reasons that we give up on self-improvement is that we establish impossible goals. See your goals as a process. This does not mean you will establish a rigid schedule for improvement or a fixed schedule for increasing time and distance. It means that you know that you will get better little by little, and so your goal is neither to run the fastest race nor to become perfect all at once. Your single, determined goal is to keep up your exercises to every extent possible, every day, day after day. Bearing in mind that you are on a path toward health, you need a diary in which you jot down landmarks along the way. Note any small things you come across, any slight increments of improvement. For example:

- Today, I walked for 10 minutes without getting winded.
- Today when I got up, I could not believe it, but I actually looked forward to my workout.
- Today while I was walking, I suddenly felt that I could face up to everything happening to me with courage and strength.

Also in your diary, answer this question: how will you know when you are getting better? When I was in chemotherapy and radiation treatment, I was very weak, yet I usually walked, with a friend who was very fit. I would have to stop and catch my breath and walk slowly, around the track sometimes, stopping altogether, while she covered many laps. My goal was not to keep up with my friend, but rather to keep on doing it. Gradually, I became better able to walk and less fearful of my cancer. Walking freed up my mind. I began to see many ways out of the trap that was mostly of my own making. The weeks when I did not improve my time or distance did not set me back, because I could see why that was not possible, given my treatment schedule. What I kept noticing was how, little by little, I was changing my whole life.

Step 3. Focus on your strengths. It is easy to beat yourself up. Some of us have honed that skill well. Instead of thinking about how you are never going to be able to exercise because you are (weak, unfit, don't know how,

82

don't have time or energy), think of which of your personal characteristics and surrounding supports would turn this into a success. Look in the mirror and tell the mirror what your strengths are. These are mine: I am a competent person. I have will and determination. I have friends/family that will support me in doing this activity. I intend to let myself be successful.

Then, and this is very important, think of a time in the past when you overcame a problem. Ask yourself what strengths you brought forward to solve this problem. Try to figure out how you could now use that same strength to solve this one. One example is that you might have called certain people for help, or you might have shown the grit to complete a task or get through a rough spot.

Step 4. Reframe the problem. One of the practices that I have employed continuously throughout this book is reframing - helping you to reframe your devastating health problem as an opportunity for growth. You have already begun to reflect on your illness in the light of having a chance to become the person you always wanted to be instead of seeing it as a curse or total disaster. Now try to reframe exercise in a way that makes it more doable and eventually will make it exciting. If you get up in the morning and think, "Another day, another boring exercise period," it will seem just like that when you are doing it. Now let's develop a thought that might turn this around. Say this to yourself:

> *I am alive today, thank heaven, and now I am going to prove it by going out for a walk. My illness has given me a golden opportunity to grow beyond the person I was before, the person whose personal health and happiness was at the bottom of a long list of things I thought were more important. My illness has set before me a challenge and a path to fulfillment. I am going to take the opportunity today to begin to know and like the person I am becoming. In exercising today, I am expressing my God-given right to health and wellbeing.*

Step 5. Learn how to change part of an unwanted pattern. All the steps above should be enough to start you off on your productive course of exercise and keep you going. But there still may be times when you just can't get unstuck. So, remember this: in order for a lifetime pattern to remain a pattern, it has to maintain itself in its entirety. If any little part of a pattern begins to crumble, then the entire pattern must adjust itself. Patterns tend to be stable and this is often good because it means that we do not have to think through every small action we take. We can rely on complex habits, built up over years. One of the problems connected with change is that people feel unnecessarily that they have to change everything at once. This is not true, nor does it usually work. Scientists who have studied patterns know that making even one small change in a large pattern will often send unwanted parts of the rest of the pattern crumbling to the ground after awhile. This especially will be true for you if you have taken seriously the steps I have outlined above.

One pattern that we all have is the sequence of things we do when we come home from work. Without really having to think about it, we each do a series of things, often in a certain order. For example you might first grab something to eat out of the refrigerator, then turn on the TV, change your clothes, make phone calls, start dinner preparations, start the laundry, or a myriad of other tasks, each of which you believe is vital, in your frantic attempt to get through your hurried day of too much work and too little time. These patterns are often well ingrained in our behavior over many years.

My colleague, Janet Allan, a nurse and anthropologist, who studies patterns of eating and exercise, believes that some of our patterns were formed when we were children. For example, grabbing something to eat when you get home from work may have started when your mother gave you an after school snack every day when you came home from school. Now, just walking in the door, makes your appetite turn on and you feel your body hungering to be fed. But there is no need to analyze where this pattern originated. Just note your pattern of behavior when you come in from work or shopping, or what you do when you get up in the morning. Then change one part of it. Stop doing one of the things you do, and replace it with one other thing that you think might be more positive.

Does that sound too easy? Well, it is easy, and also it is effective. For example, if you must grab something to eat, do it, but then don't turn on the TV. Grab your snack, and before you eat it, close your eyes and take three deep breaths. If you can work it in, do a few stretches, or a Yoga pose or two. Or pull on some walking shoes and go outdoors with the intention of walking 2 blocks, and once out there, try to do a little more. Or go outside and pull a few weeds from your garden. But please, when you start, don't try to change everything at once, just replace a few parts of your pattern with a few positive things and watch yourself begin to spend increasing time with the positive aspects of your new pattern.

Chapter 12

How To Find Yourself   Without Losing Yourself

This book was designed to teach you about four ways to prepare yourself to become a thriver and seven ways to access the support you need to become healthy. But in looking it over after it was done, I saw that it turned out to be about much more. Throughout, the spotlight is turned on examining the many ways of being authentic; how each of us can learn to live our lives with dignity and nobility, realizing that in turning around fear and taking on new ways of healthful living, we are getting closer and closer to becoming the people we have always admired.

Each chapter is a simple gift, a guide, and a highly effective tool, intended to accompany you on your personal survival journey. Remaking yourself in ways that allow you to become the very best you can be is your fierce comeback, your healthy part's response to the opportunities that uninvited illness has set on your table.

But when you change, what happens to the old you, the person you have been all your life - the parts of you that were always there - your old quilted blanket that you clung to and valued, but that did not cover you well enough in times of extreme crisis? Do you have to take a scissor to this old material or can you just add the new patches? If you do not cut out them out, will the long-standing insecurities keep reappearing in moments when you need to hold on to your newfound strong identity? Those are the questions that concerned me when at times I would seem to veer off the healthy course I was following – when I would start to rummage around the dance floor looking for another partner, forgetting about the faithful one who had brought me to the dance.

What I discovered finally was that the sweeping changes that I had made had allowed me to grow in a way that gave me an entirely different approach to my health and my life. I had a new set of principles, strengths, health habits, and ways to confront illness that stood by me and served me well. These changes promoted in me an intense inner power that unfolded as ways to live all aspects of my life, even the negative ones. But much to my consternation I discovered that the insecure and self-doubting little being that had always lived inside, was still part of me with her demands to be recognized. And worse, a frightened child was still a small patch in my quilt. So, I reasoned that maybe I had not grown in quite the same way as I thought I had.

It may seem that the advice in this book requires such enormous changes that if you adopt many or all of them, you have to turn into an entirely different person. But I do not believe that you will be that different, nor do you have to leave behind the person you were. Your change and growth toward authenticity is in the form of adding on to your repertoire of strength and knowledge, much more than eliminating what you might think of as your limitations or human weaknesses. You are not a snake. You do not shed your old skin. As you mature you do not cast yourself aside. Instead you become more and more like the ideal person that has always been living within you, waiting to be fed some nourishment and given fresh air to breathe.

That is why I do not believe for a moment that it is accurate to say that when we find ourselves experiencing old feelings and wanting to go back to old behaviors that we thought we had left behind in our newfound growth, it is because we are regressing. The person that you think you left behind is still as much an essential part of you as ever. Quite often you will feel a need to give heed to that small being that supported you for all those years without complaint. So, when that old person appears again in your life with old demands and old needs welcome him or her and attend to the requests that you feel are being presented at that moment. Sandra Cisneros, in her wonderful book, *Woman Hollering Creek,* put it this way in her chapter about a child's eleventh birthday:

> What they don't understand about birthdays and what they never tell you is that when you're eleven, you're also ten, and nine, and eight, and seven, and six and five, and four, and three, and two, and one. And when you wake up on your eleventh birthday you expect to feel eleven, but you don't. You open your eyes and everything's just like yesterday, only its today...Like some days you might say something

stupid, and that's part of you that's still ten. Or maybe some days you need to sit on your mama's lap because you're scared, and that's the part of you that's five. And maybe one day when you're all grown up maybe you will need to cry like as if you are three…Because the way you grow old is like an onion or like the rings inside a tree trunk.

So, when you vow to participate fully in life, accept that a great part of that participation is allowed because you still have access to all of parts of yourself at all your ages and stages of development. Like the five year old, some days, you may feel like sitting on your mama's lap because you are scared. The need for succor and comfort in times of crisis is an essential part of being human and living on this earth. Thank God we can acknowledge a need for being five years old again, or else we would become aloof, cold, and judgmental. It is such a mistake, in my opinion, to try to buckle up, soldier on, or be brave and stoic at times when the self is crying out its security needs. Speaking for me, there are many days when sitting in my mama's lap is exactly what I ache for. Or, feeling three, I might sit down to have a good cry. When that happens, I am required to accept the emotions that are my inherent lot as a breathing, feeling human being, so that I can welcome into my life the need for my mother's lap. I am confident that after awhile I will circle back to the dance partner that was my collaborator in the interdependent life I have developed as an adult.

I have shared a lot of my own life in this book - my fears, my insecurities, my triumphs, and my evolving beliefs. I have tried to write is as much from my heart as from my head. I have tried to picture you, the reader, as overwhelmed as I was by the sheer weight of a horribly serious diagnosis. I wanted to be with you as you struggled, as I did then, through fear and plain and unadulterated terror. I wanted to be part of your life as you went head to head with challenges that you never even dreamed about before. As I plowed through writing the book, chapter by chapter, I tried to write to you, to picture your reaction, how you might be able to take one more step if you just had this tiny piece of information that it was my privilege to give to you.

I have cared about you enough to pass on more than the spoken word of the scientific pronouncement or the latest from the experts. From my heart to yours, pours the essence of all that I have learned in my bleak and often terrible journey that was too frequently accompanied by pain and despair, but has landed here with the production of a book that I send forward to you with love.

Beverly Hall
Baltimore, Maryland
bevhall@mail.utexas.edu

References

Introduction

Frankl, V. (1959). *Man's search for meaning*. New York: Simon & Shuster.

Fromm, E. (1941). *Escape from freedom*. New York: Farr & Reinhart.

Chapter 1

Cameron E., Pauling, L. (1993). *Cancer and Vitamin C*. Philadelphia: Cameo Books.

Chapter 2

Pareles, J. (January 26, 2003). In his time of dying: Warren Zevon's last waltz. *The New York Times Magazine, 22*; 24-25.

Chapter 3

Moore, T. (1992). *Care of the soul*. New York: Harper Collins.

Selye, H. (1956). *The stress of life*. New York: McGraw-Hill.

Chapter 7

Brown, B. (1974). *New mind, new body*. New York: Harper & Row.

Crichton, M. (1988). *Travels.* New York: Alfred. A. Knopf.

Flaws, B. (1989). *Nine ounces.* Boulder, CO: New Poppy Press.

Henley, W.E. *Invictus.*

Siegel, B. (1989). *Peace, love, and healing.* New York: Harper & Row.

Simonton, O.C., Matthews-Simonton, S., Creighton, J. (1978). *Getting well again.* Los Angeles: JP Tarcher.

Chapter 8

Dossey, L. (1991). *Meaning and medicine.* New York: Bantam Books.

Krieger, D. (1981). *Therapeutic touch.* Englewood Cliffs, NJ: Prentice-Hall.

Moss, R. (1981). *The I that is we.* Berkeley, CA: Celestial Arts.

Quinn, J. (1996). *Therapeutic touch: Healing through energy fields.* NY: National League for Nursing and University of Colorado Center for Human Caring.

Chapter 9

Helminiak, D.A. (1996). *The human core of spirituality: Mind as psyche and spirit.* Albany: SUNY Press.

Lonergan, B.J.F. (1972). *Method in theology.* New York: Herder and Herder.

Noddings, N. (1984). *Caring: A feminine approach to ethics & moral education.* Berkeley: University of California Press.

Wilber, K. (1991). *Grace and grit: Spirituality and healing in the life and death of Trey Killam Wilber.* Boston: Shambhala.

Wilber, K. (1998). *The essential Ken Wilber: An introductory reader.* Boston & London: Shambhala.

Wilber, K. (1977). *The spectrum of consciousness.* Wheaton, ILL: Quest.

Interviews from my studies published in:

Hall, B.A. (1998). Patterns of spirituality in persons with advanced HIV disease. *Research in Nursing and Health*, 21, 143-153.

Hall, B.A. (1997). Spirituality in terminal illness: An alternate view of theory. *Journal of Holistic Nursing,* 15, *82-96.*

Hall, B.A. (1994). Ways of maintaining hope in HIV disease. *Research in Nursing and Health,* 17, 283-293.

Chapter 10

Angier, N. (September, 1997). Researchers find a concentrated anticancer substance in broccoli sprouts. *New York Times*. (Report of the proceedings of the National Academy of Sciences).

Balick, M. (2001). Chocolate: Healing food of the gods? *Alternative Therapies,* 7,120-122.

Dulloo, A., et al. (1999). Efficacy of a green tea extract rich in catechin-polyphenols and caffeine in increasing 25 h energy expenditure and fat oxidation in humans. *American Journal of Nutrition,* 70, 1040-1045.

Gaby, AR. (2006). Gaby's literature review and commentary. Townsend Letter. 281: 50-53.

Garland, CF et al. (2006). The role of vitamin D in cancer treatment. *American Journal of Public Health.*, 96: 252-261.

Hattersley, JG. (2006). High dose vitamin B12 for at-home prevention and reversal of Alzheimer's Disease and other diseases. Townsend Letter. 274: 91-94 & 105.

Houston, R. (2003). Two anticancer mechanisms of vitamins in humans: A review. *Townsend Letter for Doctors and Patients. June, 104-106.*

Ji, B.T., et al. (1997). Greet tea consumption and the risk of pancreatic and colorectal cancers. *International Journal of Cancer,* 70, 255-258.

Lieberman, S. Bruning, N. (2003). *The real vitamin and mineral book. New York: Avery.*

Macintosh, A. (1998). Fiber supplements: New thoughts, new choices. *Alternative & Complementary Therapies,* August, 267-275.

McCullough, Fran. (2003). *The Good Fat Cookbook.* NY: Scribner.

Pauling, L. (1986). *How to live longer and feel better.* New York: Avon.

Pittler, M.H., Ernst, E. (2000). Ginko biloba extract for the treatment of intermittent claudication: A meta-analysis of randomized trials. *The American Journal of Medicine,* 108, 276-281.

Soholm, B. (1998). Clinical improvement of memory and other cognitive functions by ginko biloba: Review of relevant literature. *Advances in Therapy,* 15, 54-65.

Spadea, L., Balestrazzi, E. (2001). Treatment of vascular retinopathies with Pycnogenol. *Phytotherapy Research,* 15, 219-223.

Chapter 11

Allan, J.D. Tyler, D. (1999). Exercise promotion. In Bulechek, G.M. & McCloskey, J.C. (eds). *Nursing interventions: Effective nursing treatments, 3rd Edition.* Philadelphia: WB Saunders, 130-147.

Berg, A.O., Atkins, D. (2002). Behavioral counseling in primary care to promote physical activity. *Annals of Internal Medicine,* 137, 205-207.

Kelder, P. (1998). *Ancient secret of the fountain of youth. Book 2.* New York: Doubleday.

Simpson, M.E. et al. (2003). Walking trends among U.S. adults. *American Journal of Preventive Medicine,* 25, 95-100.

Walker, J.L., Peller, J.E. (1992). *Becoming solution-focused in brief therapy.* New York: Brunner/Mazel Publishers.

Chapter 12

Cisneros, S. (1996). *Woman hollering creek and other stories.* New York: Random House, 6-7.

Printed in the United States
204354BV00001B/400-450/P